To Steve:  4 26, 1992

Beca___ simple acts,
like the sharing of a
meal prepared with care,
are the food that sustain
a home.
    Happy Birthday
        Love
            Jeannette

PRACTICAL THAI COOKING

PRACTICAL Thai COOKING

Puangkram C. Schmitz
Michael J. Worman

KODANSHA INTERNATIONAL
Tokyo • New York • London

Distributed in the United States by Kodansha America, Inc., 114 Fifth Avenue, New York, New York 10011.

Published by Kodansha International Ltd., 17-14, Otowa 1-chome, Bunkyo-ku, Tokyo 112 and Kodansha America, Inc.

Copyright in Japan 1985 by Kodansha International Ltd.
All rights reserved.
Printed in Japan.
First edition, 1985
Sixth printing, 1990

LCC 85-40060
ISBN 0-87011-727-0
ISBN 4-7700-1227-6 (in Japan)

Library of Congress Cataloging-in-Publication Data
Schmitz, Puangkram C.
  Practical Thai Cooking

  Includes, index.
I. Cookery, Thai. I. Worman, Michael J. II. Title
TX724.5.T5538   1985   641.5953   85-40060
ISBN 0-87011-727-0

CONTENTS

PREFACE

Years ago, whenever people learned that I was Thai, the usual response was very polite, very careful, and very blank. Mentioning *The King and I* or kick boxing often got some kind of spark, however hesitant or dim. At that time Thailand had no public image in the West. And its food was totally unknown. How different things are now.

If you mention Thailand to Americans today, the response more often than not is a happy, "Oh, Thai food." It continues to amaze me how many people in the United States enjoy Thai food, and how many consider going to a Thai restaurant a major pleasure. It seems to have happened almost overnight.

Even in Tokyo, where I live, over the years members of the foreign community asked me repeatedly to give lessons in Thai cooking. And this is a city where there is only one Thai restaurant (plus two tiny eateries), and Thai spices are completely unavailable. This is how I started classes in my own home. The demand has remained strong, and groups of about twenty people have continued for about three years now—friends, friends of friends, friends of friends of friends. . . .

Then the people at Kodansha International suggested a book. The only book specializing in Thai cooking I have encountered in American bookstores is Jennifer Brennan's excellent, bright introduction to Thai cuisine and food culture. Against this, what would be a contribution?

My answer is a no-frills approach that sidesteps culture, introductions, and explanations, directing its attention to cooking only—home cooking. Classic Thai dishes are included here (their Thai names are in parentheses below the English titles), as are adaptations and "creations." As the title states, the impulse behind this book is practicality. Thai cooking is flavor and style, not dogma.

Thai cooking also is easy. When you become familiar with the flavor vocabulary, then making Thai food becomes simple indeed. There are no fancy and fussy cooking techniques. Adding a Thai dish or two to a western meal makes both types of cooking more interesting. The dishes in this book are all ones that my family has enjoyed over the years, dishes that blend well into a western context or that can form a fully Thai meal.

Eating at a good Thai restaurant is always a pleasure. But there is no reason why Thai food must be only a restaurant experience. Here is my attempt to make Thai cooking part of the familiar fare in homes everywhere.

I want to thank my family:

My husband, Fritz, who for over twenty years has tasted and encouraged.

My son, Matthew, and my daughter, Kalina, both teenagers now. They understand. And their honesty is always a lesson and a light.

My sister, Miss Siripon Chuanchaisith—who was visiting us while the book took form—helped and kept me grounded.

My thanks to my co-author, Mike Worman, for making three languages into one and for making complexities simple.

To all my cooking students and to all the friends and guests with whom I have shared Thai food, thanks for everything said and unsaid.

To Kim Schuefftan of Kodansha International, thanks for suggesting the idea of a book, for putting it together, and for enjoying doing it.

Puang Schmitz

Tokyo
May, 1985

THAI PRONUNCIATION AND ROMANIZATION

The Thai language is a linguist's dream or nightmare, depending on how one approaches it. The aspirated and unaspirated sounds, the five tones—rising, falling, high, low, and mid—forty-eight vowels and diphthongs, all interact with diacritical marks and rules for combining this vowel with this consonant and thus changing the tones.

The novice speaker intending to say hello might well blurt out some unwitting obscenity about his listener's ancestry.

Trying to devise a romanized form that approximates the sounds of Thai is no simple matter. This is attested by street names in Bangkok. One will discover Rajdamnoen, Ratchadamnoen, and Rajdamnern for the same street on three different maps. Something as simple as beef curry may be written *gaeng nya, khaeng nua, kaeng nüa,* or *kaeng nuer*—in fact as many ways as there are cookbooks in print.

Since our interest here is food and not language, we have tried to simplify the romanized renderings of Thai words as much as possible and to use Thai words without English equivalents only where necessary. We call beef curry *gang nya.*

Anyway, pronunciation has nothing to do with preparing and enjoying this marvelous food.

BASICS

CHILI PEPPERS   Thai cooks use about ten different types of chili pepper, compared to Mexican cooks, who have over twenty to choose from.

The most common is the fiery tiny green chili called *prik kee nu*, herein called guinea peppers. (This is just a convenient English label that came from some book. It is no better or worse than "bird's-eye peppers," which also appears.) They are hotter than any Mexican variety, and care must be taken in handling them. Most cookbooks advise using rubber gloves when handling fresh guinea peppers. If you are in a hurry, be sure not to touch your eyes, nose, or the baby. The sting takes a long time to go away.

This book mainly calls for using the common Thai chili peppers that are about 3-4 inches long. Fresh, these may be yellow, green, or red; dried, they are red. The fresh may be hard to find, but the dried should be available at Southeast Asian markets. Substitute Mexican chili peppers of the appropriate size.

CHILIES IN VINEGAR (*Prik Dong Nam Som*)
MAKES 2 CUPS
    1½ cups rice vinegar
    1 Tbsp fish soy (*nam pla*)
    ½ cup chopped fresh red and green chili peppers

Wash the chili peppers and chop them into $1/_8$-inch (½-cm) pieces. Add the chopped chilies to the vinegar and fish soy and serve immediately. The essence of simplicity; this is found on every Thai table. Refrigerated, it will keep about three weeks.

CHINESE PICKLE (Tientsin Preserved Vegetable; the Chinese name translates "winter vegetable")   This pickled Chinese cabbage is usually sold in squat brown crocks or in plastic bags. One of the most common brands is Greatwall (sic), which lists Tianjin (new spelling) cabbage, salt, and garlic as ingredients. The flavor is unique; there is no substitute. Some cooks prefer to rinse the salt off before using.

COCONUT MILK AND COCONUT CREAM   Coconut milk and cream are made by soaking grated fresh or dried coconut in water, squeezing out the liquid, and discarding the coconut pulp. Coconut cream is simply richer coconut milk. The wonderfully refreshing liquid inside fresh coconuts is never used in cooking.
COCONUT MILK
    3 cups grated dried or fresh coconut
    5 cups hot or cold water (for dried or fresh coconut, respectively)
COCONUT CREAM
    3 cups grated dried or fresh coconut
    3 cups hot or cold water (for dried or fresh coconut, respectively)
Combine coconut and water in a large mixing bowl. Let sit for fifteen minutes. Mix well with your hands, then strain through cheesecloth or a fine strainer.

Economy-minded Thai housewives use the same batch of coconut to make coconut milk two or three times. This thin coconut milk is fine for soups. In Thailand, the coconut pulp is dried and fed to the chickens.

Some cooks prepare the coconut milk, let it sit for a half hour or so, and then skim off the richer liquid that rises to the top and use that as coconut cream.

Dried (or "desiccated") grated or shredded or powdered coconut available at Asian markets is excellent for making coconut milk and cream. The sweetened shredded coconut used for western baking should be avoided. Frozen fresh coconut is available and is good. Frozen coconut milk is also good. Canned coconut milk is satisfactory for some uses, but beware—it curdles. Powdered coconut milk is excellent and can be mixed to make coconut cream or milk. But by far the best and most satisfying is cream and milk made from fresh coconut. The flavors of dishes are ample testimony that opening a fresh coconut and grating or shredding the meat is worth the effort involved. A blender or food processor reduces the labor greatly.

CORIANDER   Fresh coriander is used in many cuisines throughout the world. It is found in Mexican markets, where it is called cilantro, and in Chinese markets, under the English name Chinese parsley. It is appearing more and more in supermarkets. Both leaves and root are important in Thai cooking. It is extremely difficult to estimate precise amounts—sprigs vary from small cloverlike bunches to almost celery stalk size. If serving Thai food for the first time, be cautious. There are people who find the pungent flavor of the leaves difficult (at first).

FISH SOY (*nam pla*)   This condiment is labeled "fish sauce" and "fish gravy" on some Chinese-produced bottles. The Vietnamese know this as *noc mam*, in The Philippines it is called *batis*, and in Burma it is *ngan-pya-ye*.

It is made by aging salted fish in large stone jars and filtering off the liquid.

It is indispensable to Thai cooking and is always available in Southeast Asian markets. Many supermarkets have come to stock it as a staple item.

GARLIC OIL   Chopped garlic is fried until golden (not brown) in oil over medium heat, and the garlic and oil are used together as a condiment and flavoring. A general basic proportion is 1 part garlic to 4 parts oil, by volume, though different recipes may call for different proportions.

GINGER JUICE   Probably the best way to prepare ginger juice is to finely grate fresh ginger into a dish, then place in a small piece of cheesecloth and squeeze out the juice (or just squeeze out the juice with your fingers) and discard the pulp. Cooks in a hurry pop a chunk of fresh ginger into a garlic press.

NOODLES, THIN (*Kanom Chine*)   These are fine noodles made from rice flour, as thin as the thinnest Italian vermicelli and very long.

This noodle is served with soupy curries—usually the *nam ya* type, made with shrimp, fish, or chicken. Japanese *somen* or *hiyamugi* noodles are easy to find in oriental food stores and make excellent substitutes for the Thai *kanom chine*.

serves 3-4

10-oz (300-gm) package the thicker type of Japanese *somen* noodles or *hiyamugi* noodles

Bring an ample amount of water to a rolling boil in a large saucepan over high heat. Add the noodles and cook for 4-5 minutes, stirring constantly. The noodles should be al dente. Rinse well in cold water.

PEANUTS   Use skinless roasted peanuts for all the recipes.

RICE, GLUTINOUS   This variety of rice is also commonly referred to as "sticky rice" in cookbooks, for obvious reasons, and also as "sweet rice," for unknown reasons.

To cook, soak in ample water for at least 2 hours, but preferably overnight. (Sometimes turmeric is put into the soaking water to color the rice.) Line a bamboo steamer tray with cheesecloth, get the water boiling under the steamer, and spread the soaked glutinous rice on the cheesecloth. Steam for about 15 minutes, then sprinkle with about 2 Tbsps water. Repeat this sprinkling once or twice more in the next 10 minutes. The rice should take about 30 minutes to cook. One delicious variation is to sprinkle the rice with coconut milk instead of water.

RICE, PLAIN BOILED

Long-grain rice: 1 cup rice (2 servings) needs 1¾ cups water;
3 cups (6-8 servings) rice need 5 cups water.

Short-grain (California) rice: 1 cup rice (2 servings) needs $1^1/_5$ cup water;
3 cups rice need 4 cups water.

The cooking method is the same for both types of rice:

Wash and drain the rice repeatedly, swirling it with your hand, until the washing water is clear (or nearly so). Measure the rice and water into a heavy pot with a tight-fitting lid.

Cover the pot. Bring the rice to a boil over medium-high heat and boil it for 5 minutes. Reduce the heat to low and cook the rice for 20 minutes. Turn the heat off and let the rice sit for a short time before serving.

SESAME SEEDS, TOASTING   Toast the seeds in a dry frying pan over medium heat, stirring very frequently, until the seeds just begin to pop (seven pops is the rule of thumb). Remove them from the heat immediately and spread them on a plate to cool or put into a mortar to grind. It takes only a few seconds or so for sesame seeds to scorch.

SHRIMP, DRIED

2 lbs (1 kg) very small shrimp in the shell

½ cup salt

1 cup water

Dissolve the salt in the water in a large pot. Bring the brine to a boil over high heat and add the shrimp. Cook until the water evaporates. Drain the shrimp in a colander.

Line a large cookie sheet with a kitchen towel or cheesecloth. Spread the shrimp on the cloth and dry in the sun for 2 days. Gather up the shrimp in the towel or cheesecloth and pound on a counter or table until the shells loosen. They will come off easily if they are dry. Discard the shells. If pieces of shell remain, repeat the pounding process. Return the shrimp to the sun and sun-dry for 2 more days. The important thing is to be sure the shrimp are very dry before storing them.

Alternatively, dry the shrimp several hours in a low (not hot) oven. Dried shrimp keep indefinitely in an airtight container.

SHRIMP PASTE (*kapi*)

2 lbs (1 kg) of the smallest possible shrimp

1 cup salt

Search for the tiniest available fresh shrimp—like the ones that are used for canned cocktail shrimp (but do not use canned shrimp). Wash the shrimp, but leave the shells on. Mix the salt through the shrimp thoroughly with your hands and let the shrimp stand overnight. The next day, in a mortar or food processor, pound or whir the shrimp into a fine paste. Shape the paste into a pancake 5 inches (13 cm) in diameter and 2 inches (5 cm) thick. Dry the pancake in the sun for 1 day. On the second and third days, repeat the process: break up the pancake, pound (or process) it, and shape it again each time. After the third day, put the shrimp paste in an airtight jar and age it for two months.

The finished paste will keep years without refrigeration. Keeping the ratio of shrimp to salt constant, it is easy to multiply the quantity of the recipe.

SPICES   The introduction to the Curry Pastes section (page 21) treats spices in general. We have tried to avoid really esoteric and difficult spices and ingredients. Fresh ingredients are still a problem in North America.

It is unlikely that fresh kaffir lime leaves (*bai makrut*) and peel (*makrut*) are available. Dried leaves and peel are. These can be used for simmering and flavor, but dried leaves make a dreadful garnish. Substitute fresh young lemon or orange or other citrus leaves, or just use no garnish where kaffir lime leaves are called for.

Fresh holy basil (*bai krapau*) and lemon basil (*bai manglak*) also are probably impossible. Just ignore such ingredients.

Compromises and substitutions are inevitable, but do not interfere with the quality of the dish or your cooking. If anything, they are challenges to be met creatively.

STOCKS

FISH

MAKES 10-11 CUPS

2 lbs (1 kg) fish heads, tails, bones, skin

2 stalks celery, cut into 2-inch (5-cm) lengths

10-12 peppercorns

2 whole stalks lemon grass, chopped or pounded

3-4 stalks fresh coriander, including roots, cut into 2-inch (5-cm) lengths

5 cloves garlic, chopped or pounded

1 tsp salt

Wash the fish parts and the vegetables. Place all ingredients in a large pot and add 12 cups water. Bring to a quick boil then reduce heat to medium. Simmer for 30 minutes, skimming off foam when necessary. Strain stock. Refrigerated, it keeps for 3-4 days; frozen, for several months.

CHICKEN, PORK, BEEF

MAKES ABOUT 10 CUPS

2 lbs (1 kg) chicken bones (necks, backs, etc.)

or 3½ lbs (1.5 kg) pork bones or beef bones

2 tsps salt

10 peppercorns (or ¾ tsp black pepper)

2-3 cloves garlic

½ medium onion

2 slices fresh ginger

¼ cup saké (substitute dry vermouth)

Put all ingredients in a large pot with 12 cups of water. Bring to a boil over medium heat and boil for 10 minutes. Reduce heat to low and simmer 1 hour. Strain the stock. Refrigerated, it keeps for 3-4 days; frozen, for several months.

SUGAR   In almost every recipe using sugar, ''raw sugar'' is listed. This is a substitute for palm sugar, a strong sugar made from various palm trees and common throughout Southeast Asia. The British call it ''jaggery,'' from the Hindi word. The raw sugar sold in healthfood stores is an excellent substitute. It tastes almost exactly the same and has approximately the same degree of sweetness. Or, just use regular brown sugar or granulated.

TAMARIND   This tarlike pulp from the seed pod of a large Asian tree provides a rich tartness to many Thai dishes. It is sold in packets and small jars in America.

Make tamarind water by soaking 1 Tbsp (or an equivalent glob) of tamarind pulp in ¼ cup lukewarm water for about 5 minutes. Squeeze and knead it well with your fingers to dissolve everything in the tamarind that can be dissolved, then strain out seeds and fiber. Lemon, lime, grapefruit (and even rice vinegar) will substitute.

TOFU, DRAINING   The easiest method of draining tofu is to wrap the block in a kitchen towel or cheesecloth and weight it with 2 dinner plates or a small cutting board for about 10-30 minutes, depending on how firm you want the tofu.

UTENSILS   No fancy equipment is needed to cook Thai food. A wok is excellent, but a large frying pan will do. If you are going to do a lot of Thai cooking, a heavy mortar and pestle (stone, if possible) are great tools that do certain things well (handling small quantities and certain tough, dried spices, as discussed elsewhere). Also, pounding spices and ingredients such as peanuts releases flavors, aromas, and oils. This does not happen in electric whiz machines.

A steamer is also necessary for some dishes, but, if you do not own one, this can be improvised with a large pot.

(top to bottom) Pork and Liver Salad (p. 70); Red Curry with Shrimp and Pineapple (p. 114); Spicy Tofu Salad (p. 80)

(left to right) Deep-Fried Tofu with Peanut Sauce (p. 51); Three-Color Seafood Salad (p. 77); Spicy Tomato Soup (p. 63); Sardines with Mint (p. 118); Stir-Fried

Sweet-and-Sour Vegetables (p. 90); Thai Crepe Rolls (p. 53); (center) Baked
Chicken and Mushrooms in Coconut Milk (p. 126)

(top to bottom) Chuck Roast with Sour Curry (p. 146); Stuffed
Peppers—Thai Style (p. 85); Son-in-Law Eggs (p. 97)

(top to bottom) Mussels with Sour Curry (p. 111); Snow Peas with
Scallops (p. 91); Barbecued Chicken, Thai Style (p. 132)

(left to right) Stir-Fried Shrimp with Lemon Grass (p. 115); Chicken and Potato Balls (p. 49); Chicken and Coconut Soup with Galanga (p. 57); Cold Noodles with Shrimp and Pineapple (p. 160); Masaman Curry with Beef (p. 147)

(top to bottom) Three-Color Glutinous Rice Balls (p. 171); Bananas in Coconut Cream (p. 167); Glutinous Rice and Bananas (p. 172); Steamed Custard in Winter Squash (p. 170)

CURRY PASTES

เครื่องแกง

A quick glance through this cookbook will reveal that most dishes call for so many teaspoons or tablespoons of some curry paste. The recipes for these pastes are not complicated. All the curry paste recipes require either a mortar and pestle (found in every Thai kitchen) or a blender or food processor. Though each of the latter two saves much labor, a mortar works best for small quantities and for fibrous dried ingredients, especially dried lemon grass, which do not break down easily in the blender or food processor, even after lengthy soaking.

A blender or food processor will suffice when a fibrous material is called for if one of the below is followed:

1. Fish out any lumps or pieces of dried spice from the completed dish after cooking and before serving.

2. Whir the curry *sauce* (without the solid main ingredients) in a blender or food processor after cooking, on the assumption that all hard spices have gotten soft. This assumption is not always right, and methods of preparation do not always allow this.

3. Probably the best measure is to choose dried spices that are as fresh as possible, something that is not always easy to tell. In general, avoid hard, thick lumps. For example, galanga and *grachai* slices or strips should break easily and have a certain delicacy of texture, not resemble bits of desert-baked shoe.

When using dried spices, it will be necessary to add a little water (a teaspoon or two at a time) to get enough moisture to form the pastes, even if the spices have been soaked until soft. Soaking water is excellent for this purpose.

Pastes made from dried spices will keep in an airtight container in the refrigerator for about two weeks, and indefinitely in the freezer. Pastes made from fresh ingredients will not keep well unless fried briefly in oil over medium heat. To do this, use 4 parts curry paste to 1 part oil, by volume; add a pinch of salt. If cooked in this way, they may be refrigerated indefinitely in an airtight jar. Pastes burn if fried at too high a heat or for too long.

The issues of fresh versus dried ingredients and of small batches versus large quantities are ones each cook solves individually. The flavor of pastes and dishes made with fresh or fresh-frozen spices will quickly convince one that such fresh ingredients are worth searching out. Dried spices are easily available in Southeast Asian markets, as are prepared curry pastes of all kinds. The latter tend to be very hot. These will do, but once you start making your own pastes, you will not be satisfied with the prepared ones.

A glance at the ingredients of the various pastes gives the impression that they are composed of roughly the same things. Though this is generally true, proportions vary a great deal, and the differences in flavor are distinct, not clever or too subtle. Follow the recipes exactly at first, then start experimenting on your own. It will not be long before you find what you and your family and friends like.

♨ Green Curry Paste
(Gang Keo Wan)

This is a widely used paste good for fish, poultry, beef, and pork curries.

MAKES ABOUT ½ CUP

12 fresh green chili peppers, coarsely chopped
1½ Tbsps chopped garlic
1½ Tbsps chopped fresh lemon grass (or 2 Tbsps powdered)
1 Tbsp chopped fresh galanga (or 2 Tbsps dried)
1 Tbsp chopped fresh kaffir lime peel (or 2 Tbsps dried)
1 Tbsp chopped coriander root
1 tsp caraway seeds
1 tsp ground turmeric
1 tsp salt
1 tsp shrimp paste (**kapi**)

Soak all dried ingredients until sufficiently soft.

Place all ingredients in a blender or food processor and whir to form a smooth paste. If using dried ingredients, it may be necessary to add water in small amounts; use the soaking water of any of the dried ingredients.

Or, pound to a paste with a mortar and pestle.

♨ Traditional Masaman (Muslim) Curry Paste
(Gang Masaman)

This is the basis for the wonderful Masaman Beef Curry, so popular with westerners. Thai cardamom is milder than the Indian. The presence of this spice indicates the curry's Indian origin, hence the name.

MAKES ½–⅔ CUP

12 dried red chili peppers, seeded, soaked, and coarsely chopped
2 Tbsps coriander seeds
2 tsps ground cumin
1 tsp ground nutmeg
1 tsp ground mace
seeds of 10 cardamoms
4 bay leaves
1 tsp ground cinnamon
1 tsp ground cloves
12 small cloves garlic, coarsely chopped
10 shallots, chopped (substitute red onion)
6-8 peppercorns, whole or freshly ground
2 slices fresh galanga (or 4 slices dried)
2 whole stalks fresh lemon grass, finely chopped (or 2 Tbsps powdered)
1 tsp shrimp paste (**kapi**)

Soak all dried ingredients until sufficiently soft.

Place all ingredients in a blender or food processor and whir to form a smooth paste. If using dried ingredients, it may be necessary to add water in small amounts to allow a paste to be formed; use the soaking water of any of the dried ingredients.

Or, pound to a paste with a mortar and pestle.

♠ Simple Masaman (Muslim) Curry Paste
(*Gang Masaman*)

Here is a simple version of the traditional paste (preceding recipe).

MAKES ABOUT ⅔ CUP

12 dried red chili peppers, seeded, soaked, and coarsely chopped

2 Tbsps coarsely chopped garlic

1 Tbsp chopped fresh lemon grass (or 2 Tbsps dried)

1 Tbsp peanut oil

2 Tbsps chopped shallots (substitute red onion)

1 Tbsp sugar

1 Tbsp salt

¾ tsp ground cumin

¾ tsp ground cardamom

Soak all dried ingredients until sufficiently soft.

Place all ingredients in a blender or food processor and whir to form a smooth paste. If using dried ingredients, it may be necessary to add water in small amounts in order to make a paste; use the soaking water of any of the dried ingredients.

Or, pound to a paste with a mortar and pestle.

♠ Red Curry Paste
(*Gang Pet*)

This paste lends itself to seafood, poultry, and beef. It is used in regular curries and also in dry, sautéed meat mixtures.

MAKES ABOUT ¾ CUP

12 dried red chili peppers, soaked and coarsely chopped

1 Tbsp coarsely chopped fresh lemon grass (or 1½ Tbsps powdered)

1 Tbsp chopped fresh galanga (or 2 Tbsps dried)

2 tsps coriander seeds

1 tsp caraway seeds

2 Tbsps chopped garlic

1 tsp shrimp paste (*kapi*)

1 Tbsp chopped fresh kaffir lime peel (or 2 Tbsps dried)

2 Tbsps chopped shallots (substitute red onion)

Soak all dried ingredients until sufficiently soft.

Place all ingredients in a blender or food processor and whir to form a smooth paste. If using dried ingredients, it may be necessary to add water in small amounts; use the soaking water of any of the dried ingredients.

Or, pound to a paste with a mortar and pestle.

♠ Yellow Curry Paste
(*Gang Luang No. 1*)

Used for vegetable, seafood, chicken, and pork dishes.

MAKES ABOUT ½ CUP

12 dried red chili peppers, seeded, soaked, and coarsely chopped

5 tsps chopped shallots (substitute red onion)

1 Tbsp chopped coriander root

1 Tbsp chopped fresh lemon grass (or 1½ Tbsps powdered)

1 Tbsp ground cumin

5 tsps ground turmeric

1 Tbsp peanut oil (or vegetable oil)

Place the chilies, shallots, coriander root, and lemon grass in a blender or food processor and whir to make a smooth paste. Add the remaining ingredients and whir until smooth.

Or, proceed in the same manner with a mortar and pestle.

♠ Orange Curry Paste
(*Gang Luang No. 2*)

MAKES ABOUT ½ CUP

12 dried red chili peppers, seeded, soaked, and coarsely chopped

2 Tbsps coarsely chopped garlic

1 Tbsp chopped fresh turmeric (or 1½ Tbsps powdered)

1 Tbsp coarsely chopped fresh lemon grass (or 2 Tbsps powdered)

1 Tbsp salt

1½ Tbsps shrimp paste (*kapi*)

Place the chilies, garlic, turmeric, and lemon grass in a blender or food processor and whir to form a smooth paste. Add the salt and shrimp paste and blend again.

Or, follow the same procedure with a mortar and pestle.

▲ Korat Curry Paste
(*Gang Korat*)

This very hot paste is used for seafood, poultry, and meat dishes.

MAKES ABOUT ½ CUP

14 dried red chili peppers, seeded, soaked, and coarsely chopped
2 Tbsps chopped fresh lemon grass (or 3 Tbsps powdered)
1 tsp chopped fresh galanga (or 2 tsps dried)
¼ cup chopped shallots (substitute red onion)
1½ tsps shrimp paste (*kapi*)
1 tsp chopped fresh *grachai* (*Kaempferia pandurata*)
1 tsp peppercorns, whole or freshly ground
1 tsp chopped fresh kaffir lime peel (or 2 tsps dried)
½ tsp salt

Soak all dried ingredients until sufficiently soft.

Place all ingredients in a blender or food processor and whir to form a smooth paste. If using dried ingredients, it may be necessary to add water in small amounts. Use the soaking water of any of the dried ingredients.

Or, pound to a paste with a mortar and pestle.

▲ Choo Chee Curry Paste
(*Gang Choo Chee*)

This paste is used for seafood.

MAKES ABOUT ⅔ CUP

12 dried red chili peppers, seeded, soaked, and coarsely chopped
1 Tbsp chopped coriander root
2 Tbsps chopped garlic
1 Tbsp shrimp paste (*kapi*)
1 Tbsp chopped fresh galanga (or 2 Tbsps dried)
1 Tbsp chopped fresh lemon grass (or 1½ Tbsps powdered)
1 Tbsp chopped shallots (substitute red onion)
1 tsp salt

Soak the dried ingredients until sufficiently soft.

Place all ingredients in a blender or food processor and whir to form a smooth paste. It may be necessary to add water in small amounts if dried ingredients are used; use the soaking water of such ingredients.

Or, pound to a paste with a mortar and pestle.

♨ Gang Ba (Country) Curry Paste
(Gang Ba)

This general-purpose paste is used for all curries—vegetable, seafood, chicken, pork, and beef.

MAKES ABOUT ¾ CUP

13 dried red chili peppers, seeded, soaked, and coarsely chopped

2 Tbsps chopped shallots (substitute red onion)

1 Tbsp chopped garlic

1 Tbsp chopped fresh galanga (or 2 Tbsps dried)

1½ Tbsps fresh kaffir lime peel (or 3 Tbsps dried)

1 Tbsp grated lemon rind

1½ Tbsps chopped fresh lemon grass (or 2 Tbsps powdered)

1 tsp finely chopped fresh ginger

Soak all dried ingredients until sufficiently soft.

Place all ingredients in a blender or food processor and whir to form a smooth paste. If dried ingredients are used, it may be necessary to add small amounts of water to make the paste smooth; use the soaking water of any of the dried ingredients.

Or, pound to a paste with a mortar and pestle.

♨ Sour Curry Paste
(Gang Som)

This curry paste by itself is not sour, but it is used with other sour ingredients like tamarind water, vinegar, tomato, etc., in cooking.

MAKES ABOUT ¾ CUP

10 dried red chili peppers, seeded, soaked, and coarsely chopped

1½ Tbsps coarsely chopped fresh lemon grass (or 2 Tbsps powdered)

3 Tbsps chopped shallots (substitute red onion)

2 Tbsps shrimp paste (kapi)

1 Tbsp sugar

Place all ingredients in a blender or food processor and whir to make a smooth paste.

Or, pound to a paste with a mortar and pestle.

♠ Nam Ya Curry Paste
(Gang Nam Ya)

This paste is the basis for many fish curries and can be used with any white-fleshed fish or the white meat of chicken.

MAKES ABOUT 2 CUPS

6–8 dried red chili peppers, seeded, soaked, and coarsely chopped
¼ cup chopped shallots (substitute red onion)
1 Tbsp chopped garlic
2 tsps chopped fresh galanga (or 4 tsps dried)
¼ cup chopped fresh lemon grass (or 6 Tbsps powdered)
1 tsp chopped fresh kaffir lime peel (or 2 tsps dried)
2 tsps shrimp paste (*kapi*)
1 cup chopped fresh (or dried) *grachai* (*Kaempferia pandurata*)
    (there is no substitute)
1 tsp salt

Soak the dried ingredients until sufficiently soft.

Place all ingredients except the last two in a blender or food processor and whir until the mixture is a smooth paste. Add the salt and blend until smooth. If using dried ingredients, small amounts of water may be needed to make a paste; use the soaking water of such ingredients.

Or, pound to a smooth paste with a mortar and pestle.

♠ Peppery Curry Paste
(Prik King)

Although this is called a "curry paste," it is not used in curries. It is used to enhance the flavor of stir-fried meat, poultry dishes, and seafood.

MAKES ABOUT 1½ CUPS

12–15 dried red chili peppers, seeded, soaked, and coarsely chopped
1 tsp finely chopped fresh kaffir lime peel (or 2 tsps dried)
4 tsps chopped coriander root
1 tsp salt
1 tsp peppercorns, whole or freshly ground
1 tsp chopped fresh galanga (or 2 tsps dried)
1 tsp chopped fresh lemon grass (or 2 tsps powdered)
1 tsp chopped garlic
½ cup chopped shallots (substitute red onion)
½ cup dried shrimp, rinsed

Soak all dried ingredients until sufficiently soft.

Place all ingredients in a blender or food processor and whir until a smooth paste is formed. If dried ingredients are used, small amounts of water may be necessary for a paste to be formed. In that case, use the soaking water of such ingredients.

Or, pound to a smooth paste with a mortar and pestle.

♨ Gang Liang Curry Paste
(*Gang Liang*)

This paste is used for many vegetable curries, especially those including cauliflower, spinach, corn, squash, or pumpkin.

MAKES ABOUT 1 CUP

6 dried red chili peppers, seeded, soaked, and coarsely chopped

1 Tbsp peppercorns, whole or freshly ground

½ cup chopped shallots (substitute red onion)

1 Tbsp shrimp paste (*kapi*)

¼ cup chopped fresh (or ½ cup dried) *grachai* (*Kaempferia pandurata*) (there is no substitute)

¾ cup dried shrimp, rinsed and chopped

Soak any dried ingredients until sufficiently soft.

Place all ingredients in a blender or food processor and whir to make a smooth paste. If dried ingredients are used, small amounts of water may be needed to allow a smooth paste to be made; use the soaking water of such ingredients for this purpose.

Or, pound to a smooth paste with a mortar and pestle.

♨ Panang Curry Paste
(*Panang*)

This marvelous paste is considered by some to be the finest Thai flavor. Unlike most Thai curries, the panangs are almost dry, whether made with beef, pork, chicken, or fish.

MAKES ABOUT 1 CUP

12–15 dried red chili peppers, seeded, soaked, and coarsely chopped

¼ cup chopped shallots (substitute red onion)

¼ cup chopped garlic

2 Tbsps chopped fresh lemon grass (or 3 Tbsps powdered)

1 Tbsp chopped fresh galanga (or 2 Tbsps dried)

1 Tbsp chopped fresh kaffir lime peel (or 2 Tbsps dried)

1 tsp ground mace

1 tsp cardamom seeds (removed from the pods)

1 tsp peppercorns, whole or freshly ground

1 Tbsp chopped coriander root

2 tsps caraway seeds

2 tsps shrimp paste (*kapi*)

1 tsp salt

Soak any dried ingredients until sufficiently soft.

Place all ingredients in a blender or food processor and whir to make a smooth paste. Small amounts of water may be needed to make a smooth paste if dried ingredients are used; use the soaking water of such ingredients.

Or, pound to a smooth paste with a mortar and pestle.

SAUCES AND DIPS

น้ำ พริก — หลน

Chili sauces are ubiquitous in Thailand. They are eaten in one form or another in the poorest hut and the grandest palace. An essential part of Thai cooking, these pungent flavors complement equally well boiled rice and intricate fish, meat, or vegetable dishes. The sauces accompany vegetables—usually raw, but sometimes lightly cooked—as a dip. They also act as dips for grilled foods such as fish and poultry, and as flavor additives in numerous dishes.

They are put together in a matter of minutes and are of seemingly infinite variety. The most common ingredients are shrimp paste, garlic, fish soy, a sour ingredient such as tamarind water or lime or lemon juice and, of course, chili peppers. As with curry pastes, a blender or food processor is marvelous for soft ingredients, but for small amounts and some dried spices, a sturdy mortar and pestle are the cook's most efficient tools.

If exotic sour ingredients are unavailable, substitute any sour fruit such as green mangos, unripe plums or apricots, or even grapefruit or cooking apples.

Serve these sauces with all vegetables—raw, simmered in coconut milk, lightly steamed or parboiled, or even fried. The only word of caution, which cannot be repeated too often, is do not overcook them.

♠ All-Purpose Chili Sauce
(*Prik Dong*)

This sauce is not used by itself but is an additive that enlivens almost any dish, especially stir-fried and meat dishes. It is marvelous added to spaghetti sauce, lasagne, ratatouille—whatever you like—and simple dishes like stir-fried vegetables come alive with just a touch.

MAKES ABOUT 2½ PINTS

1 lb (½ kg) fresh or dried red chili peppers, washed and dried completely
2 cups vinegar (rice vinegar is best)
½ cup sugar
⅓ cup salt
⅓ cup saké (substitute sweet white wine)
1 cup garlic cloves

If using dried chili peppers, soak them in the vinegar for half an hour. Peel the garlic but do not wash it. Place all ingredients in a blender or food processor and whir until a coarse paste is formed.

The flavor of this all-purpose Thai sauce is best when made with the freshest possible red chilies in the fall. The longer you keep it, the more the flavor will mature.

♠ Red Chili Sauce
(*Nam Prik Dang*)

This simple sauce is good with parboiled or raw vegetables such as asparagus, okra, cucumber, broccoli, and cauliflower.

MAKES ABOUT 1 CUP

A INGREDIENTS
5 dried red chili peppers, grilled until crisp
6 shallots, grilled until just brown, then peeled
4 cloves garlic, grilled until just brown, then peeled
1 Tbsp shrimp paste (*kapi*)
2 Tbsps anchovy paste
¼ lb (115 gm) trout fillet(s), grilled until lightly browned

2 Tbsps oil

B INGREDIENTS
2 Tbsps fish soy (*nam pla*)
1 tsp sugar
2 Tbsps tamarind water (see page 12; substitute lime juice)

Place the A INGREDIENTS in a blender or food processor and whir until a coarse paste is formed. Heat the oil in a frying pan or wok and add the paste. Stir-fry over low heat for 5 minutes. Add the B INGREDIENTS and adjust the flavor to suit your taste—sweeter, more sour, or saltier.

▲ Mango Chili Sauce
(Nam Prik Mamaung)

This versatile sauce is good as a dip for raw vegetables such as cucumbers, carrots, green beans, and fresh mushrooms. It can also be used to top lightly boiled vegetables.

MAKES ABOUT 2 CUPS

1 medium-sized, hard, green mango
½ cup dried shrimp, rinsed
1 Tbsp chopped garlic
5 fresh green chili peppers
1 tsp shrimp paste (*kapi*)
1½ Tbsps fish soy (*nam pla*)
1 tsp sugar (optional)
1 tsp chopped fresh coriander leaves

2 Tbsps coarsely chopped or crushed peanuts

Peel the unripe mango and shred it rather finely with a grater or food processor. Whir the softened shrimp, garlic, green chilies, and shrimp paste in a blender or food processor to a coarse paste. (Or pound with a mortar and pestle.) Add the shredded mango and blend gently. (Do not allow it to become too smooth.) Mix in the fish soy, sugar, and coriander leaves and adjust the flavor to taste. Place in a serving dish and sprinkle with crushed peanuts before serving.

▲ Tamarind Chili Sauce
(Nam Prik Ma Kam)

This sauce is good as an accompaniment to stir-fried beef and pork dishes as well as a dip for vegetables.

MAKES ABOUT 1⅓ CUPS

1 cup fresh tamarind (substitute green tomatoes or very sour cooking apples)
5 shallots, coarsely chopped
1½ Tbsps coarsely chopped garlic
15–20 guinea peppers (*prik kee nu*)
1 Tbsp shrimp paste (*kapi*)
1–1½ Tbsps fish soy (*nam pla*)
2 tsps raw sugar
2–3 Tbsps vegetable oil
½ cup dried shrimp, rinsed

Wash the fresh tamarind and chop it coarsely. Combine the tamarind, shallots, garlic, guinea peppers, and shrimp paste in a mortar and pound into a very rough paste. (It is probably not wise to use a blender or food processor, because if the paste becomes too smooth, the distinctness of the flavors will be lost.)

Add the fish soy and sugar. Blend gently.

Put the vegetable oil in a frying pan and heat it over low heat. Add the rough paste and sauté it for 2 or 3 minutes.

Pound the ½ cup of dried shrimp very roughly and mix into the paste.

♠ Shrimp and Grapefruit Chili Sauce
(*Nam Prik Kung*)

This sauce is usually used for vegetables that have been cooked in coconut milk. Typical choices would include fresh green beans, Chinese cabbage, cauliflower, and carrots.

MAKES ABOUT 1⅓ CUPS

10–12 fresh green or yellow chili peppers, seeded and coarsely chopped

10–12 fresh red chili peppers, seeded and coarsely chopped

1 Tbsp shrimp paste (*kapi*)

5 oz (150 gm) fresh shrimp, shelled and deveined

½ cup shredded grapefruit sections

2–3 Tbsps fish soy (*nam pla*)

2 tsps sugar

GARNISH

1 Tbsp chopped fresh coriander leaves

Whir all the chilies, the garlic, and the shrimp paste until smooth in a blender or food processor or pound in a mortar.

Grill the shrimp under a hot broiler and dice them. Mix the shrimp and shredded grapefruit sections with the paste.

Add the fish soy and sugar. Adjust the seasoning to taste at this point.

Place in a serving dish and sprinkle with coriander leaves. Some bright red chilies on top add interest.

♠ Traditional Bean Paste Dip
(*Tou Chiaw Lon*)

This is much milder than the various chili sauces.

MAKES ABOUT 3½ CUPS

2 tsps coarsely chopped coriander root

5 peppercorns, whole or freshly ground

1 Tbsp coarsely chopped garlic

¾ cup white (sweet) bean paste (Chinese or Japanese)

2½ cups coconut cream

¼ lb (115 gm) ground pork

3 oz (90 gm) finely chopped fresh shrimp

2 Tbsps tamarind water (see page 12)

1 Tbsp sugar

¼ tsp salt (optional)

GARNISHES

⅓ cup thinly sliced shallots (substitute red onion)

3 fresh red chili peppers, cut into fine slivers

Combine the coriander root, peppercorns, and garlic in a blender or food processor and whir to form a paste (or pound with a mortar and pestle). Add the white bean paste and blend 2 or 3 minutes to make a very smooth paste.

Heat ½ cup of the coconut cream over medium heat and add the paste. Cook until the aroma is released—about 1 minute. Add the pork and shrimp and cook, stirring constantly, for 3 minutes. It is important not to leave the paste at this time, or it will form a hard ball. Add the remaining 2 cups of coconut cream and the tamarind water, sugar and salt (optional). Reduce the heat to low and cook for 10 minutes.

Remove to a serving bowl and sprinkle with sliced shallot and chili slivers just before serving.

♠ Shrimp Paste Dip
(Kapi Lon)

MAKES ABOUT 3 CUPS

3–4 dried red chili peppers, seeded, soaked, and coarsely chopped

1½ Tbsps chopped fresh lemon grass (or 2 Tbsps powdered)

2 Tbsps chopped shallots (substitute red onion)

2½ cups coconut milk

½ cup high-quality shrimp paste (kapi)

¼ lb (115 gm) fresh shrimp, blended or pounded into a smooth paste

1 Tbsp fish soy (nam pla) (optional)

1 Tbsp sugar

GARNISH

1 fresh red chili pepper, cut into fine slivers

Place the chilies, lemon grass, and shallots in a blender or food processor and whir to make a coarse paste (or pound in a mortar).

Put ½ cup of the coconut milk in a saucepan over low heat. Add the chili-lemon grass shallot paste, the shrimp paste, and the shrimp and simmer for 5 minutes. Taste the mixture and adjust the seasoning with fish soy and sugar.

Add the remaining 2 cups of coconut milk and continue to simmer for 10

minutes. The dip will be very soupy. Cool to room temperature.
  Garnish with slivers of red chili pepper.

♠ Satay Sauce

This sauce accompanies the Thai Satay recipe on page 49.

MAKES ABOUT 2⅔ CUPS

A MIXTURE

3 large fresh chili peppers, coarsely chopped

3 shallots, coarsely chopped

2 cloves garlic, coarsely chopped

2 slices fresh (or dried and soaked) galanga, coarsely chopped

B MIXTURE

1 Tbsp chopped fresh lemon grass (or 1½ Tbsps powdered)

1 Tbsp coriander seeds

¼ tsp ground mace

¼ tsp ground nutmeg

¼ tsp ground cinnamon

2 cups coconut milk

1½ Tbsps raw sugar

3 Tbsps tamarind water (see page 12)

1½ Tbsps fish soy (*nam pla*)

⅓ cup white sesame seeds

1½ cups coarsely chopped or crushed peanuts

GARNISH

1 Tbsp chopped fresh coriander leaves

Place all A MIXTURE ingredients in a dry frying pan and cook over low heat, stirring constantly, just until they begin to change color. Remove from heat. In a blender, food processor, or a mortar, make the A and B MIXTURES into a smooth paste.

  Place ½ cup of the coconut milk in a frying pan and heat it over medium heat. Add the paste and stir until the aroma is released—about 1 minute. Add the remaining 1½ cups coconut milk, bring to a boil over medium heat, and boil gently for 3 minutes. Add the sugar, tamarind water, and fish soy. Simmer for 4 more minutes and use these last 3 ingredients to adjust the flavor to taste. Remove from heat.

  Toast the white sesame seeds (see page 12) and grind them roughly in a mortar. Add the peanuts and the sesame seeds to the sauce. Let the sauce cool. Place in a serving dish and sprinkle with coriander leaves before serving with the satay (page 49). Serve at room temperature.

Variation

In place of the paste made of the A and B MIXTURES in this recipe, you can use 2–3 Tbsps of *Masaman* Curry Paste (page 23).

♠ Roasted Chili Sauce
(Nam Prik Pow)

This multipurpose sauce is used for vegetables, stir-fried dishes, seafood, and tofu dishes. For a unique blend of East and West, try it on a chicken, beef, or pork sandwich instead of butter or mayonnaise. It is also essential for Sour Prawn Soup, the hot soup on page 60. The name is a direct translation from the Thai, but, as can be seen below, ingredients are not roasted, but deep-fried. This keeps almost indefinitely refrigerated.

MAKES ABOUT 2 CUPS

A MIXTURE

3 Tbsps tamarind water (see page 12)

3 Tbsps fish soy (nam pla)

1 tsp salt

2 Tbsps shrimp paste (kapi)

3 Tbsps sugar

1½ cups vegetable oil for deep-frying

B MIXTURE

¾ cup garlic cloves

1 cup shallots (substitute red onion)

½ cup dried shrimp

¾ cup dried red chili peppers, seeded, soaked, and coarsely chopped

Blend the ingredients of A MIXTURE and set aside.

Heat the oil to 360° F/180° C and deep-fry the garlic until it starts to brown. Remove the garlic and add the shallots to the oil. Deep-fry them until they begin to turn brown. Remove the shallots and add the shrimp to the oil. Deep-fry the shrimp for 2–3 minutes. Remove the shrimp and add the chilies. Deep-fry the chilies just until they begin to darken. This happens very quickly. Take care not to burn. Reserve the chilies, then strain the oil and reserve.

Make the B MIXTURE into a paste by whirring in a blender or food processor or pounding in a mortar.

Return ½ cup of the oil to the pan, add the A and B MIXTURES, and simmer over low heat for 15 minutes, stirring occasionally. Cool to room temperature.

♠ Coriander Chili Sauce
(Nam Prik Pak Chee)

Like so many other sauces and dips, this is good with raw string beans, carrots, cucumbers, or lightly cooked squash. Unlike the others, when accompanied by a cooling beer and a bowl of plain white rice, it makes a pleasant meal.

1 Tbsp shrimp paste (*kapi*)
1 Tbsp coarsely chopped garlic
½ cup dried shrimp, rinsed and roughly pounded
5–6 fresh red chili peppers, coarsely chopped

1–2 Tbsps chopped fresh coriander leaves
2 Tbsps fish soy (*nam pla*)
2–3 tsps sugar
2 Tbsps lime juice

OPTIONAL
more fresh chili peppers, coarsely chopped
more dried shrimp, rinsed and roughly pounded
more chopped fresh coriander leaves

Cook the shrimp paste in a dry (no oil) frying pan over low heat until it releases its aroma—a few seconds only. Pound or blend it with the garlic, dried shrimp, and fresh chilies to a smooth paste. Add the coriander leaves, fish soy, sugar, and lime juice and taste. It should be a rough combination of hot, sour, sweet, and salty flavors. Correct the flavor by adding any of the OPTIONAL ingredients until you are satisfied.

SNACKS

อาหารว่าง

Anyone who spends more than a day in Thailand will likely agree
with the observation that the Thai people may be the snackingest
people on the globe. They simply eat whenever the urge strikes.

Street vendors are everywhere in the cities, while boats ply the
rivers and canals, selling noodles, grilled bananas, grilled meats
with cucumber pickles, fruits, candies, and confections. A quick
walk through any market reveals countless tempting snacks—hot
and cold, spicy and bland, sweet and salty. Snacks generally are
vendor food, not home cooking.

In the traditional Thai household, hors d'oeuvres before a meal
or as part of a cocktail party are unknown. Snacks generally know
no time limit. Minutes after breakfast and several times throughout
the day and into the night Thais grab a handful of nuts, a bit of
dried sweet meat, a cookie, a fried banana, and so on and so on.

The snacks included here all adapt themselves to western enter-
taining. That is, they make fine additions to a buffet table or work
well as hors d'oeuvres.

♠ Thai Corn Cakes

This is good as a snack or as a side dish in a western or Thai meal.

SERVES 6–8

3 cups corn, fresh off the cob (or frozen)

2 eggs, beaten

2 Tbsps cornstarch

1 cup fresh shrimp (substitute equal volume of chicken breast)

2 tsps coarsely chopped coriander root

1 tsp coarsely chopped garlic

4 peppercorns, whole or freshly ground

1 tsp sugar

1–1½ Tbsps fish soy (*nam pla*)

½ cup vegetable oil for frying

If using frozen corn, thaw and chop coarsely. If cutting the corn off the cob, do so in 3 slices, not just one close to the cob—the resulting kernels will be the right size. Add the egg and cornstarch to the corn.

Shell and devein the shrimp and chop coarsely. (If using chicken, chop it into pieces as small as the corn kernels.)

Pound the coriander root, garlic, peppercorns, sugar, and fish soy to a paste in a mortar. Add shrimp and this paste to the corn and egg mixture and mix well. Adjust seasoning.

Pour some of the oil in a frying pan or on a griddle over medium-high heat. When the oil is hot, fry pancakes of the corn mixture about 3 inches (8 cm) in diameter and ¼-inch (¾-cm) thick. Brown on both sides, turning only once.

♠ Golden Shrimp Toast
(*Ka Nom Pang Na Gung*)

MAKES 40 PIECES

10 slices thinly sliced sandwich bread (white, rye, or whole wheat)

1 lb (450 gm) medium shrimp, shelled and deveined

5 peppercorns, whole or freshly ground

2 coriander roots, coarsely chopped

1 clove garlic, coarsely chopped

¼ tsp salt

2 green onions, chopped

1 egg, well beaten

2–3 cups vegetable oil for deep-frying

2 more eggs, well beaten

Trim off crusts from the 10 slices of bread and cut bread into quarters (like diamonds if you are feeling fancy).

Coarsely chop or pound the shrimp in a mortar. Set aside. Also in a mortar, pound the pepper, coriander, garlic, and salt to a thick paste. (There is not enough volume to use a blender or food processor for this.) Place the mixture in a bowl and add the chopped green onion, 1 beaten egg, and shrimp. Beat by hand until frothy and light—about 5 minutes.

Spread the paste evenly on the 40 pieces of bread and set aside. Heat the oil in a wok or frying pan to hot (360° F/180° C) over medium-high heat. Dip the shrimp-coated bread in the 2 well-beaten eggs, and deep-fry, shrimp side down, until golden.

Serve hot as an hors d'oeuvre with either of the Cucumber Pickles (see page 73).

▲ Fried Wonton

Anyone familiar with Chinese food will recognize these as purely Chinese in origin, with the coriander root and fish soy being Thai flavors.

MAKES 40 WONTON

5 coriander roots, coarsely chopped

2–3 cloves garlic, coarsely chopped

5 peppercorns, whole or freshly ground

1 Tbsp cornstarch

2 Tbsps water

1½ Tbsps fish soy (*nam pla*)

1⅓ lbs (600 gm) ground pork

2 eggs, lightly beaten

5 green onions, finely chopped

40 prepared wonton wrappers

2–3 cups vegetable oil for deep-frying

In a blender or food processor, whir the coriander roots, garlic, peppercorns, cornstarch, water, and fish soy to form a paste (or pound in a mortar). Add the pork, egg, and chopped green onions and mix well.

Place 1 tsp of the mixture in the center of a wonton wrapper. Moisten two opposite corners with water, bring these corners together and pinch firmly. (It is more attractive if the tips of the corners do not align exactly.) Fold the remaining 2 corners toward the center. Continue until all the wrappers are used. It is convenient to place the prepared wonton on a cookie sheet.

In a wok or deep-fryer, heat the vegetable oil to hot (360° F/180° C) over medium-high heat and deep-fry the wonton until golden. Serve hot with Cucumber Pickle A (see page 73).

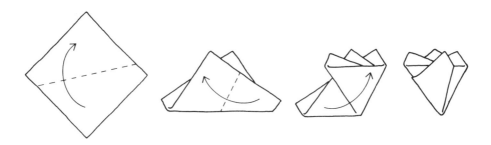

Variation
Substitute shrimp, crab, or a combination of the two for the pork.

▲ Hot Thai Sandwiches (Beef, Pork, Chicken)

MAKES 40 PIECES

10 slices sandwich bread (white, rye, or whole wheat)

SEASONINGS
1–2 Tbsps Red Curry Paste (see page 24)
2 Tbsps chopped fresh coriander leaves
½ cup finely chopped or crushed peanuts
2 green onions, chopped
1 kaffir lime leaf (*bai makrut*), finely chopped
½ tsp salt
½ tsp sugar

2 cups ground meat—beef, pork, or chicken

4 Tbsps vegetable oil

2 eggs, beaten
1 Tbsp fish soy (*nam pla*)

lettuce leaves

Trim the crusts off the bread.
   Mix the SEASONINGS, then add the ground meat and mix.
   Put the vegetable oil in a frying pan over medium heat. When the oil is hot, add the meat mixture and stir-fry for 5 minutes. Add the beaten eggs and fish soy and stir-fry 2 more minutes.
   Wash and pat dry the lettuce. Cover each bread slice with a lettuce leaf. Spread some of the meat mixture on top. Cut into quarters (or diamonds) and serve hot as an hors d'oeuvre or snack.

♠ Steamed Meatballs

This is a Thai adaptation of a famous Chinese dish, which is called such names as "snowballs" or "pearls" in cookbooks. It does, in fact, look marvelous on a buffet or dinner table.

MAKES 30 MEATBALLS

1½ cups glutinous rice, washed and soaked overnight

A MIXTURE

4 dried shiitake mushrooms, soaked for 30 minutes

1½ cups ground pork

1 cup coarsely chopped fresh shrimp

4 green onions, chopped

B MIXTURE

½ tsp coarsely chopped coriander root

1 clove garlic, coarsely chopped

1 Tbsp fish soy (*nam pla*)

½ tsp pepper

½ tsp sugar

Drain the glutinous rice well.

Trim off the stems of the soaked shiitake mushrooms and chop the caps very fine. Combine the A MIXTURE and mix well.

Pound the B MIXTURE ingredients in a mortar to form a smooth paste.

Combine A and B MIXTURES and blend.

Make small meatballs about 1 inch (2 cm) in diameter and roll them in the well-drained glutinous rice. Arrange the balls in a steamer and steam them over medium heat for about 30 minutes, or until the glutinous rice is done. Serve hot with any of a wide variety of piquant sauces—Worchestershire sauce, Chinese hot mustard, English mustard, a soy sauce and vinegar mix, etc.—or just as they are without any accompaniments.

♠ Banana Chips
(*Gluay Charp*)

MAKES A BIG BATCH
(enough to give away, probably)

2 lbs (1 kg) underripe bananas

3 cups vegetable oil for deep-frying

1 cup coconut milk (or water)

2 lbs (1 kg) sugar

½ tsp salt

Peel the bananas and slice them as thin as potato chips. (Clearly, anyone without a food processor will not make this.)

In a wok or large frying pan, heat the oil to hot (360° F/180° C) over medium-high heat. Deep-fry the banana chips until they are crisp and golden. Drain well on absorbent paper.

Place coconut milk (or water), sugar, and salt in a saucepan and make a syrup over low heat by cooking for 10 minutes, until thick.

Turn the heat off and add the banana chips. Coat them with the syrup, taking care not to break the chips. They will dry to resemble sugar-coated breakfast cereal.

Keeps extremely well (nothing lasts forever) in an airtight jar.

♠ Dried Bananas
(*Gluay Dak*)

These are perfect for hikers and campers since the flavor does not change but the weight is reduced by half.

MAKES PLENTY

2 lbs (1 kg) not quite ripe bananas (smaller bananas are good for drying)

1 Tbsp salt

3 cups water

Peel the bananas. Dissolve the Tbsp salt in the 3 cups water. Add bananas and soak for 1 hour. Drain. Dry in the sun on a cookie sheet for 3 days. Keep bananas as clean as possible while sun-drying.

Flatten the bananas somewhat by placing a cutting board on top and pressing down with your hand. They should be about ½-inch (1-cm) thick.

Sun-dry 3 more days.

After a total drying time of 6 days, the bananas will be half their original size and will be light brown. Store in an airtight jar. Will keep 3 or 4 weeks.

♠ Thai Spring Rolls

MAKES 20 ROLLS

7 peppercorns, whole or freshly ground

3 cloves garlic, coarsely chopped

3 coriander roots, coarsely chopped

3–4 Tbsps vegetable oil

1 cup fresh or canned crab meat, cartilage removed

¼ lb (115 gm) Chinese sausage, cut into julienne strips

**2 oz (60 gm) saifun noodles, soaked 5 minutes in warm water
    and cut into 1½-inch (4-cm) lengths**

¼ cup julienned bamboo shoots

2 Tbsps fish soy (*nam pla*)

1 Tbsp sugar

1 Tbsp cornstarch dissolved in 2 Tbsps water

¼ cup fresh chopped coriander leaves

20 spring roll wrappers
2–3 cups vegetable oil for deep-frying

Make the peppercorns, garlic, and coriander roots into a paste in a blender or food processor (or mortar). Heat the 3–4 Tbsps vegetable oil in a frying pan or wok. Add the paste and stir-fry over medium heat until it releases its aroma—a few seconds only. Add the crab, julienned sausage, pork, saifun noodles, and bamboo shoot and stir-fry for 3–5 minutes. Add the SEASONINGS and stir-fry an additional 3–5 minutes. Turn the heat off and sprinkle with coriander leaves.

Separate the spring roll wrappers. Place a wrapper with a narrow side facing you. Place a scant ¼ cup of the filling about one-third of the way from the closest edge. Fold the closest edge over the filling, then fold over the right and left edges, then roll. Depending on the texture of the wrappers, you may need to seal the end with water or egg yolk mixed with water. Continue with all the filling and place the finished rolls, seam side down, on a cookie sheet until ready to fry. Do not let them touch each other, or they will stick together.

In a wok or deep-fryer, heat the 2–3 cups of vegetable oil to hot (360° F/180° C) over medium-high heat and deep-fry the spring rolls on both sides until golden.

Serve very hot with Cucumber Pickle B (see page 73).

▲ Vegetarian Spring Rolls

MAKES 30 ROLLS

12 oz (360 gm) regular tofu (Japanese "cotton" tofu)
4–5 dried shiitake mushrooms, soaked 30 minutes in tepid water, stems trimmed off
¼ lb (115 gm) green beans
1 stalk celery
½ medium carrot
2 green onions

3 Tbsps vegetable oil
1 Tbsp finely chopped garlic
½ tsp black pepper
2 Tbsps Red Curry Paste (see page 24)
2–3 tsps fish soy (*nam pla*)

30 spring roll wrappers

3 cups vegetable oil for deep-drying

Cut the tofu, mushroom caps, green beans, celery, and carrots into large julienne pieces 1½ inches (4 cm) long. Chop the green onions, including the tops, into 1½-inch (4-cm) lengths.

Put the 3 Tbsps vegetable oil in a frying pan or wok over medium heat. When the oil is hot, add the garlic and stir-fry just until it begins to brown. Add the pepper and curry paste and stir-fry until the aroma is given off—just a few seconds. Add the fish soy, tofu, and all vegetables except the green onions. Stir-fry the mixture about 10 minutes, turn the heat off, and add the green onions.

Separate the spring roll wrappers and prepare the spring rolls in the same manner as in the preceding recipe (Thai Spring Rolls).

In a wok or deep-fryer, heat the oil to hot (360° F/180° C) over medium-high heat and deep-fry the rolls on each side until golden. Drain well and serve hot with the Cucumber Pickle B (see page 73) for a hearty vegetarian snack or hors d'oeuvre.

♨ Chicken and Potato Balls
(color pages 18–19)

SERVES 6–8

2 cups finely chopped cooked chicken breast meat
2 cups diced cooked potatoes

5 oz (150 gm) fresh shrimp, shelled, deveined, and finely chopped
½ onion, finely chopped
2 eggs, well beaten
2 Tbsps Red Curry Paste (see page 24)
¼ tsp salt
2 Tbsps fish soy (nam pla)
3 Tbsps vegetable oil
3 green onions finely chopped
2 Tbsps chopped fresh coriander leaves

2 cups dry bread crumbs
3 cups vegetable oil for deep-frying

Mash the potatoes coarsely with a fork. Place mashed potatoes, chicken, and shrimp in a mixing bowl. Mix in the chopped onion, beaten egg, curry paste, salt, fish soy, and 3 Tbsps vegetable oil, chopped green onion, and coriander leaves.

Form into walnut-sized balls. Roll the balls in bread crumbs to coat well. Fry in hot (360° F/180° C) oil until golden. Drain.

Serve hot with any piquant sauce of your choice and/or Cucumber Pickle A (see page 73). This must be eaten hot because the flavor fades rapidly when it cools.

▲ Thai Satay

MAKES 20 SKEWERS

2 lbs (1 kg) boneless chicken meat (breast is best), skin removed and reserved
1½ Tbsps curry powder
½ tsp salt
1 Tbsp sugar
½ cup coconut milk
1 Tbsp rice vinegar (or any mild vinegar)
another ½ cup coconut milk
20 bamboo skewers (about 5 in/13 cm long)

Skin the chicken, wash it, and pat it dry. Cut the meat into ⅛ × 1 × 4-inch (½ × 2 × 10-cm) pieces. Cut the skin into 1-inch (2-cm) squares. Mix the curry powder, salt, and sugar. Add this to the chicken strips and chicken skin and marinate for 5 minutes. Add the first ½ cup of coconut milk and mix thoroughly. (Use your hands.) Add the vinegar and marinate the chicken for at least 1 hour at room temperature.

Thread the skewers using first a piece of chicken meat and then a piece of chicken skin. Broil over a hot charcoal fire until cooked through—turning only once. After turning, sprinkle some of the second ½ cup of coconut milk on the meat.

Serve at once with Cucumber Pickle A (see page 73) and Satay Sauce (see page 37).

Variations
Thinly sliced beef or pork can replace the chicken, or use a combination of all three meats.

▲ Fish and Potato Patties

SERVES 6–8

1 lb (450 gm) sole fillets
3 cups coarsely mashed potatoes
½ onion, finely chopped
3 Tbsps vegetable oil

SEASONINGS
½–1 tsp pepper
2 Tbsps chopped fresh coriander leaves
¼ tsp salt
1½ Tbsps fish soy (*nam pla*)
1 egg, lightly beaten

2 eggs, well beaten
2 cups coarsely crushed corn flakes

2 cups vegetable oil for deep-frying

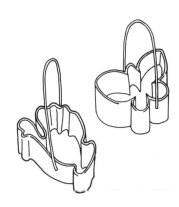

chopped green onions
red chili peppers, cut into fine slivers

Wash the sole fillets and cut them into ¼-inch (¾-cm) chunks. Boil the fish chunks over high heat for 2 minutes in just enough lightly salted water to cover. Drain and cool.

Mix the fish and mashed potatoes together, add the chopped onion, 3 Tbsps vegetable oil, and all the SEASONINGS. Mix well.

Spread the mixture on a cutting board to form a 1½-inch (4-cm) thick layer. Using fancy cutters (see sketch and *Note* below), shape the patties into chickens, eggs, and fish.

In a wok or deep-fryer, heat the 2 cups oil to hot (360° F/180° C) over medium-high heat. Dip the patties into the beaten egg and then into the crushed corn flakes. Deep-fry until both sides are golden. Sprinkle with garnishes.

Serve with Cucumber Pickle A (see page 73) as part of a buffet or an attractive hors d'oeuvre.

Note: If you do not have the fancy cutters, simply shape the mixture into round or oval patties. They taste the same.

♠ Deep-Fried Tofu with Peanut Sauce
(Tow Hoo Tod)
(color page 14)

If you have access to a large oriental market, you will be able to find tofu that has already been deep-fried. (It is called nama age *in Japanese.) Or, use regular ("cotton") tofu, wrap it in a clean kitchen towel, and press under two dinner plates for about an hour. This will rid it of water and make it firm.*

SERVES 6–8 AS AN APPETIZER

1 lb (450 gm) deep-fried tofu (Japanese: *nama age*) (substitute regular tofu)

2 cloves garlic, coarsely chopped
1 coriander root, coarsely chopped
3 dried red chili peppers, seeded, soaked, and coarsely chopped
½ tsp salt
¾ cup rice vinegar (cider vinegar is fine)

¼ cup sugar
½ cup finely chopped or crushed peanuts

2 cups peanut oil (or vegetable oil)

GARNISHES
2 tsps chopped fresh coriander leaves
2 tsps red pepper flakes

Cut the tofu in 1 × 1 × 1½-inch (2 × 2 × 4-cm) pieces. Set aside.

Make a paste (with such small quantities, a mortar and pestle are probably the easiest method) of the garlic, coriander root, 3 seeded chili peppers, and salt. Add the vinegar and mix.

Dissolve the ¼ cup of sugar in ¼ cup hot water and add it to the paste along with the ½ cup of chopped peanuts. Mix well and put in a serving bowl. Sprinkle with coriander leaves and red pepper flakes.

Put the 2 cups of peanut (or vegetable) oil in a wok or frying pan over medium-high heat. Deep-fry the deep-fried tofu in hot (360° F/180° C) oil for 1 minute (the fresh tofu for 5 minutes), until a light gold. Drain on paper towels.

Place the tofu on a serving plate and the bowl of peanut sauce next to it. Use the peanut sauce as a dip. Serve either hot or at room temperature.

▲ Thai Style Fried Tenderloin

SERVES 6–8 AS AN APPETIZER

2 lbs (1 kg) beef tenderloin

SEASONINGS
1 Tbsp coarsely chopped coriander root

2 Tbsps coarsely chopped garlic

2 tsps peppercorns, whole or freshly ground

¼ cup red wine

2 tsps coriander seeds

2 Tbsps fish soy (*nam pla*)

1 Tbsp sugar

¼ cup cornstarch

2 cups vegetable oil for deep-frying

Cut the tenderloin into ⅛ × 1 × 2-inch (½ × 2 × 5-cm) pieces. This is easier if you put the meat in the freezer for about 2 hours then cut it across the grain. (Or ask your butcher to do it.)

Blend all SEASONINGS in a food processor or blender to a paste. Mix with the beef and marinate at room temperature for 1 hour or in the refrigerator for 1 day.

Just before frying, add the ¼ cup cornstarch and mix well with your hands. Heat the oil to hot (360° F/180° C) in a wok or frying pan and deep-fry the marinated beef for about 5 minutes, until it is well done.

Serve at room temperature as a snack or part of a buffet dinner. After it has been fried, this will keep for at least a week in the refrigerator.

▲Thai Crepe Rolls

(*Gwit Dio Lod*)
(color page 14)

This Chinese-inspired dish can be found in many versions throughout Southeast Asia. Here is a Thai version—good for breakfast, lunch, or snacks. The filling—with an added dash of the All-Purpose Chili Sauce on page 33—can be used to stuff pita bread.

SERVES 4–6

1 Tbsp vegetable oil

4 eggs

3 Tbsps flour

FILLING

2 oz (60 gm) fresh bean sprouts

2 Tbsps vegetable oil

1 Tbsp finely chopped garlic

¼ lb (115 gm) shredded cooked chicken

¼ lb (115 gm) chopped cooked shrimp

3 green onions, chopped into 1½-inch (4-cm) lengths

½ tsp salt

¾ tsp pepper

GARNISHES

red chili peppers, cut into fine slivers

chopped green onions

chopped fresh coriander leaves

For the crepes, beat the eggs well with ½ cup water then blend in the 1 Tbsp oil and 3 Tbsps flour. Heat a frying pan over medium heat, oil very lightly, and add just enough of the batter to make a crepe about 5–6 inches (13–15 cm) in diameter. Fry on one side only until firm. The bottom will be browned. Set aside and make 10–11 more, until batter is gone. Or, use already prepared Chinese pancakes (*bao bin*).

Clean the bean sprouts, place them in a bowl, and pour boiling water on them. Let sit for 1 minute, then plunge into cold water to refresh. Put 2 Tbsps oil in a wok over medium heat, add the garlic, and stir-fry until golden. Add the chicken, shrimp, bean sprouts, green onion, and salt and pepper. Stir-fry over medium heat for 2 minutes. Let cool to room temperature.

To assemble the rolls, place 1½ Tbsps of FILLING on a pancake and simply roll up. Serve at room temperature.

Arrange the finished rolls seam side down on a serving plate and garnish with chili slivers, chopped green onion, and chopped fresh coriander leaves. Almost any kind of sauce or dip, such as Red Chili Sauce (see page 33) or Chilies in Vinegar (see page 9) goes well with these, as does regular American or hot Chinese mustard.

▲ Galloping Horses—Spiced Meat on Pineapple
(Ma Ho)

This famous and attractive Thai dish is a snap to prepare.

SERVES 6–8

1½ Tbsps coarsely chopped garlic
1½ tsps coarsely chopped coriander root
1 tsp saké
16 peppercorns, whole or freshly ground

4 Tbsps vegetable oil

10 oz (300 gm) lean ground pork (substitute ground chicken)
5 oz (150 gm) shrimp, chopped coarsely

SEASONINGS
2 Tbsps fish soy (*nam pla*)
1½ Tbsps raw sugar
¾ cup peanuts, coarsely chopped or crushed

1 large ripe pineapple, peeled

GARNISHES
3 fresh (or dried) red chili peppers, seeded and cut into fine slivers
whole fresh coriander leaves

Make the garlic, coriander roots, saké, and peppercorns into a paste in a blender or food processor or with a mortar and pestle. Add the vegetable oil to a frying pan over medium heat. Add the paste and stir-fry until the aroma is released—a few seconds. Add the pork and shrimp and stir-fry until cooked. Break up the meat with a fork or spatula while it is cooking.

Add the SEASONINGS and fry until the sugar is blended into the meat mixture. Remove from heat and let the mixture cool in the pan.

Slice the pineapple into ½-inch (1-cm) thick rings and cut the rings into ½ × 1½-inch (1 × 4-cm) chunks.

Put a small amount of the cooled meat mixture on each pineapple chunk. Pinch off individual coriander leaves. Decorate each "galloping horse" with a few slivers of chili and a coriander leaf. These make a very attractive hors d'oeuvre.

Variations
Vegetarians can substitute fresh shiitake mushrooms for the pork or chicken. Navel orange slices or even firm avocado slices can take the place of the pineapple.

SOUPS

แกงจืด

Soups are an integral part of Thai cuisine. *Thom yam* soups (with shrimp, pork, chicken, or mixed seafood) are not easily forgotten. The bold combination of lemon grass, lemon juice, and kaffir lime leaves with meat or fish and chili peppers leaves an indelible impression on the taste buds. Of course, the amount of chili pepper can be adjusted, but once accustomed to this typical Thai taste, one forgets it was ever thought to be too hot.

In sharp contrast to the spicy *thom yam* soups are the subtle and delicious *gang chud*, literally, "bland curries." These are made of simple stock with a vegetable (cabbage, daikon radish, or spinach) base and maybe a small bit of fish or meat. These quiet soups are wonderful accompaniments to very hot curries.

▲ Saifun Noodle and Meatball Soup
(*Gang Chud Wun Sen*)

SERVES 6–8

1 oz (30 gm) saifun noodles (Chinese type preferred; Japanese *harusame* gets mushy)
4 dried shiitake mushrooms
6 cups pork stock (see page 12)
2 Tbsps fish soy (*nam pla*)

MEATBALLS
5 oz (150 gm) ground pork
1 small clove garlic, finely chopped
½ tsp black pepper
1 Tbsp fish soy (*nam pla*)
2 green onions, chopped

10 oz (300 gm) regular tofu (Japanese "cotton" tofu), cut into ½ × ½ × 1½-inch
    (1 × 1 × 4-cm) pieces

GARNISH
1 Tbsp chopped fresh coriander leaves

CONDIMENTS
garlic oil (see page 10)
Chinese pickle (Tientsin Preserved Vegetable)

Soak the saifun noodles in hot water for 10 minutes. Cut into about 3-inch (8-cm) lengths. Reconstitute the dried shiitake mushrooms in warm water for 30 minutes, remove stems, and cut caps into fourths. (You can add the mushroom soaking water to the soup stock for additional flavor.)

Place the soup stock and fish soy in a soup pot and bring to a rapid boil. Meanwhile mix the MEATBALL ingredients and form into bite-sized meatballs. (Making them perfectly round is not so important.)

Drop the meatballs and mushrooms into the boiling stock and cook over medium heat for 5 minutes. Add the noodles and tofu and cook for 3 more minutes. Divide the soup among 6 or 8 bowls. Season with a little black pepper and sprinkle some chopped coriander leaves on each bowl.

Place small bowls of garlic oil and Chinese pickle on the table and let people season their own soup. Serve hot.

▲ Chicken and Coconut Soup with Galanga
(*Gai Tom Ka*)
(color page 19)

The flavors of coconut milk and galanga are wonderfully Thai. The chicken can be light meat or dark, with or without bones and skin—suit yourself.

6–8 slices fresh or dried galanga

5–6 whole stalks fresh lemon grass, cut into 3-inch (8-cm) lengths
   (or 7–8 stalks dried, soaked 30 minutes and chopped)

8 peppercorns

5 cups coconut milk

2 lbs (1 kg) chicken, cut into ½ × ½ × 1-inch (1 × 1 × 2-cm) pieces

SEASONINGS

juice of 1 lime (or ½ lemon)

3 Tbsps fish soy (*nam pla*)

½ tsp sugar

3–5 fresh red chili peppers, either slivered or pounded

GARNISHES

2 Tbsps chopped fresh coriander leaves

4–5 fresh kaffir lime leaves (*bai makrut*), torn into shreds (optional)

Put the galanga, lemon grass, peppercorns, coconut milk, and 1 cup of water into a soup pot. Bring to a boil over medium heat and add the chicken. Simmer over low heat for 15 minutes or until the chicken is tender. Remove the whole spices (lemon grass, galanga, and peppercorns). Add the SEASONINGS. Although not recommended for this soup, if you really like things hot, you can increase the chilies.

Remove to soup bowls and sprinkle with coriander and kaffir lime leaves before serving.

▲ Shrimp Ball Soup

SHRIMP BALLS

⅓ lb (150 gm) fresh shrimp

¼ lb (115 gm) ground chicken breast

1 tsp coarsely chopped garlic

¼ tsp pepper

3 coriander roots, coarsely chopped (or 1 Tbsp chopped coriander leaves)

1 Tbsp fish soy (*nam pla*)

2 tsps cornstarch

SOUP

8 cups stock (chicken or pork; see page 12)

2 Tbsps fish soy (*nam pla*)

1 can straw mushrooms (substitute 3 oz/90 gm fresh button mushrooms)

⅓ lb (150 gm) Chinese cabbage

SEASONINGS

1 Tbsp garlic oil (see page 10)

2 green onions, cut into 1-inch (2-cm) lengths
black pepper
2 Tbsps chopped fresh coriander leaves

Shell and devein the shrimp and whir in food processor or blender with the chicken and other SHRIMP BALL ingredients until smooth.

Place the soup stock and fish soy in a saucepan. Cut the mushrooms in half and cut the Chinese cabbage into 1-inch (2-cm) pieces and add both to the stock. Bring to a boil over high heat and quickly drop the shrimp ball mixture into the boiling stock, 1 Tbsp at a time. Add the SEASONINGS and cook until shrimp balls rise to the top. Serve hot.

(If you cannot find Chinese cabbage, you can substitute lettuce, but add it after the soup is in the bowls. Do not cook it at all.)

♠ Mild Lemon Soup with Chicken and Mushrooms

This delicate soup goes well with a western meal.

SERVES 6–8

½ lb (225 gm) boneless chicken breast

1 Tbsp saké
2 egg whites, lightly beaten
¼ tsp white pepper
¼ tsp salt
2 Tbsps cornstarch

7 cups chicken stock (see page 12)
5 oz (150 gm) fresh straw mushrooms (or 1 can straw mushrooms;
    substitute button mushrooms)
1 clove garlic, crushed

SEASONINGS
3 green onions, cut into 1½-inch (4-cm) lengths
2 Tbsps fish soy (*nam pla*)
dash white pepper
juice of ½ lemon
½ Tbsp vegetable oil (optional)

Wash the chicken breast and cut it across the grain into very thin bite-sized pieces. Marinate it in the saké for 10 minutes. Then add the egg white, pepper, salt, and cornstarch and mix to coat the chicken pieces evenly.

Bring chicken stock to a boil over medium heat. Add mushrooms and garlic and the marinated, cornstarch-coated chicken. Bring the soup to a boil again and boil for 2 minutes. Remove from heat and add SEASONINGS all at once. Stir gently and adjust seasoning to taste. Serve hot.

♠ Sour Prawn Soup
(*Tom Yam Gung*)

This is by far the most typical of Thai soups. The flavor strength here has been toned down a bit. If you prefer the authentic, increase the chilies and the lemon juice. Recently, excellent Tom Yam *cubes (like bouillon cubes) have become available, evidence of this soup's popularity.*

SERVES 6–8

SOUP

1–2 slices dried galanga, soaked for 20 minutes

3 whole stalks fresh lemon grass, lightly pounded in a mortar
    (or 5 stalks dried, soaked and chopped)

2 fresh (or dried) kaffir lime leaves (*bai makrut*)

2 medium-sized stalks coriander with roots

5–7 guinea peppers (*prik kee nu*), lightly pounded in a mortar

1 Tbsp Roasted Chili Sauce (see page 38)

6 cups chicken stock (see page 12)

10 oz (300 gm) medium shrimp, shelled and deveined

5 oz (150 gm) fresh straw mushrooms, cut in half (substitute button mushrooms)

SEASONINGS

2 Tbsps fish soy (*nam pla*)

1–2 tsps sugar

juice of small lemon

GARNISH

chopped green onion tops

Place all the SOUP ingredients in a soup pot over medium heat and boil for 5 minutes. Add the shrimp and mushrooms and just return to a boil. (If you overcook the shrimp, they will become rubbery.) Mix in the SEASONINGS.

Pour the soup into 6 or 8 bowls. Sprinkle with chopped green onion tops before serving.

Variations
An equal amount of sliced chicken or sukiyaki style beef can be used instead of shrimp. The cooking time is exactly the same.

♠ Tofu Soup with Lemon Grass

This soup is hot! For a less fiery version, eliminate the guinea peppers (these are the reason why it is hot) and add chilies or not as you like.

SERVES 6–8

1 lb (500 gm) regular tofu (Japanese "cotton" tofu)

2 cups fresh straw mushrooms (substitute any fresh mushrooms)

A SEASONINGS

3–4 slices fresh or dried galanga

2 coriander roots, coarsely chopped

3 whole stalks fresh or dried lemon grass, cut into 3-inch (8-cm) lengths

3–5 fresh (or dried) kaffir lime leaves (*bai makrut*)

2½ Tbsps fish soy (*nam pla*)

B SEASONINGS

5 guinea peppers (*prik kee nu*), each smashed once with a hammer
    (or 5 red chili peppers, chopped)

1–1½ Tbsps Roasted Chili Sauce (see page 38)

2–3 Tbsps lime or lemon juice

½ tsp sugar (optional)

GARNISHES

2 green onions, chopped

2 Tbsps chopped fresh coriander leaves

Cut the tofu into ½-inch (1-cm) cubes. Cut the mushrooms in half.

Put 6 cups cold water in a large saucepan and bring to a rapid boil. Add the A SEASONINGS, reduce heat to medium-low, and simmer for 15 minutes. Remove any solid pieces of galanga, coriander root, lemon grass, and kaffir lime leaf. Add the tofu and mushrooms and simmer 3 more minutes. Mix in the B SEASONINGS and heat through.

Place in a soup tureen and sprinkle with chopped green onion and fresh coriander.

Variation

Use 6 cups of fish stock (see page 12) in place of water and omit the A SEASONINGS.

♠ Rice Soup with Seafood
(*Kaw Tom Pla*)

Leftover rice is fine to use in this dish. If shrimp and fish get boring, use your favorite seafoods. Squid, oysters, clams, crab—all are excellent.

SERVES 6

2 cups long-grain rice, washed

7 cups water

1 Tbsp vegetable oil (for stir-frying)

5 oz (150 gm) medium shrimp, shelled and deveined

5 oz (150 gm) firm white-fleshed fish, cut into 1-inch (2-cm) squares

2 Tbsps garlic oil (see page 10)

½ tsp pepper

3 Tbsps fish soy (*nam pla*)

½ cup julienned celery

2 Tbsps Chinese pickle (Tientsin Preserved Vegetable; optional)

GARNISH

chopped fresh coriander leaves or chopped green onion tops

Bring the water to a boil over medium heat and add the rice. While it is cooking, cut the fish.

Stir-fry shrimp and fish 1 minute in 1 Tbsp oil over high heat.

When the rice is cooked but not soft (about 15–18 minutes), add the fish and shrimp and all the remaining ingredients, including the garlic oil.

Place soup in individual bowls and sprinkle with fresh coriander or green onion tops before serving. Serve hot. Keeps 2 days refrigerated. Good reheated.

▲ Tofu and Meatball Soup
(Gang Chud Too Hoo)

SERVES 8

MEATBALLS

⅓ lb (150 gm) ground pork

1 clove garlic, finely chopped

¼ tsp white pepper

pinch of salt

1 tsp saké

2 tsps cornstarch

1 green onion, finely chopped

8 cups soup stock (chicken or pork; see page 12)

12 oz (360 gm) regular tofu (Japanese ''cotton'' tofu)

2 oz (60 gm) button mushrooms, cut in half

SEASONINGS

2 Tbsps fish soy (nam pla)

1 Tbsp Chinese pickle (Tientsin Preserved Vegetable)

2 green onions, cut into 1-inch (2-cm) lengths

1 Tbsp chopped fresh coriander leaves

Mix all the MEATBALL ingredients and set aside.

Place the soup stock in a pot and bring to a boil over medium heat. Drop the meatball mixture into the boiling soup stock about ½ Tbsp at a time. Return to a low boil and cook for 5 minutes.

Cut the tofu into ½ × 1 × 1-inch (1 × 2 × 2-cm) pieces. Add mushrooms and tofu to the boiling stock. Bring to a boil again and add the SEASONINGS.

Place soup in individual soup bowls and sprinkle with a dash of black pepper. Serve piping hot.

♠Clear Soup with Daikon Radish

This very easy, clear soup goes well with western dishes. Good clear soup stock can be made from the bones of roast chicken or ham. To keep the stock clear, the bones must be simmered over very low heat for a long time. Rapid boiling will make the stock cloudy.

SERVES 8

9 cups chicken stock (see page 12)
5 oz (150 gm) lean salt pork (substitute cooked ham), cut into thick julienne strips
2-inch (5-cm) piece (about ½ lb/225 gm) daikon radish, cut into julienne strips
3 Tbsps fish soy (*nam pla*)

SEASONINGS
¼ tsp white pepper
1 Tbsp Chinese pickle (Tientsin Preserved Vegetable)
2 green onions, chopped
1 Tbsp chopped fresh coriander leaves

Place the soup stock in a pot and add the meat, julienned daikon, and fish soy. Cook over medium heat for 15 minutes or until both the meat and daikon are tender. Add the SEASONINGS and adjust to taste.

♠ Spicy Tomato Soup
(color page 15)

This ordinary looking soup will surprise and delight the blasé diner. It is not ordinary. Good with a hearty meal.

SERVES 6–8

2 15-oz cans stewed tomatoes
5 oz (150 gm) cooked white-fleshed fish
3 cups coconut milk
½–1 Tbsp Red Curry Paste (see page 24)
2 Tbsps fish soy (*nam pla*)
1 Tbsp lemon juice

GARNISH
2 Tbsps chopped fresh coriander leaves or chopped green onion tops

Puree the tomatoes in a blender or food processor. Set aside. Then puree together the fish and the coconut milk.

Put the tomatoes, blended fish and coconut milk, curry paste, fish soy, and lemon juice in a soup pot. Bring to a boil over medium heat, reduce heat to low, and simmer for 10 minutes. Sprinkle with fresh coriander leaves or chopped green onion tops before serving.

Variation
Vegetarians can substitute tofu for the fish.

▲ Shrimp Soup with Lime

This simple soup can take the place of the traditional Sour Prawn Soup (page 60) when you do not have lemon grass or galanga on hand.

SERVES 6–8

⅔ lb (300 gm) medium shrimp
7 oz (200 gm) button mushrooms, cut in half

SOUP
6 cups chicken stock (see page 12)
1 Tbsp saké
2 cloves garlic, crushed
1 small leek, cut in 1½-inch (4-cm) lengths (celery is also good)
2 Tbsps fish soy (*nam pla*)

SEASONINGS
3 Tbsps lime juice
½ tsp red pepper flakes
1 Tbsp chopped fresh coriander leaves

Shell shrimp, leaving tails intact. Slit down the back and devein.

Bring the SOUP ingredients to a boil over high heat. Add shrimp and mushrooms, bring to a boil again, and cook only 1 minute. Add the SEASONINGS and serve.

Variation
Replace the shrimp with 12 oz (360 gm) tofu, cut into 1-inch (2-cm) cubes.

▲ Spicy Beef Soup
(*Tom Yam Nya*)

SERVES 6–8

10 oz (300 gm) round steak cut into very thin slices (sukiyaki style)
1 Tbsp rosé wine
5 oz (150 gm) button mushrooms, sliced
5 cups beef stock (see page 12)
3–5 dried red chili peppers, seeded and cut lengthwise into 4–5 pieces
5 shallots
3 cloves garlic
3 coriander roots (substitute 3 stalks celery)
2 Tbsps fish soy (*nam pla*)
1 tsp sugar
juice of ½ lemon or lime
1 Tbsp Roasted Chili Sauce (see page 38) (substitute ¼ tsp
    chopped fresh red chili pepper)

2 green onions, chopped
5–7 guinea peppers (*prik kee nu*), crushed lightly

Cut the thinly sliced meat into 1 × 1½-inch (2 × 4-cm) pieces. Marinate the meat in the wine for 10 minutes. Put the 5 cups beef stock in a soup pot. Add the dried red chili peppers.

Flatten the shallots, garlic, and coriander roots by smashing with the side of a cleaver or with a hammer. Chop very coarsely. (If using celery, cut it into 1½-inch/4-cm pieces and flatten it in a similar way.)

Add all the smashed vegetables to the soup with the fish soy and sugar. Bring to a boil over medium heat and boil for 3 minutes. Remove all solid ingredients to make a clear soup and bring to a boil again. Now add the meat and the mushrooms. Reduce the heat to low and add the lemon (or lime) juice and chili sauce. Adjust the seasonings—the soup should be sour, sweet, and salty. If you like it even hotter, add more chili sauce (or chopped fresh chili pepper).

Place in individual bowls or a soup tureen and sprinkle with chopped green onion and crushed guinea peppers.

SALADS

ยำ

It is only natural that salads are important in the hot, sticky climate of Thailand. Virtually all meals in Thailand are accompanied by some kind of salad—as simple as a handful of raw green beans to go with a fiery curry or as complex as the meat-seafood-vegetable extravaganzas that restaurants love to show off.

Salads can be meals in themselves or parts of a large repast. Unlike America, where salads come at the start of the meal, or France, where diners cleanse the palate with them in the middle, in Thailand, salads do not have a fixed position. They are part of the whole and are served along with everything else.

The range of ingredients used in Thai salads is much greater than that used for salads in the West. It is in salads, that the Thai art of decorative cutting and carving of vegetables can be shown off.

♠ Bean Sprout Salad with Ham and Chicken

This salad is a good excuse to use leftover ham and chicken—in fact, it was invented for that purpose. If meat is not the mood, try cooked fish or shrimp.

SERVES 6–8

½ lb (225 gm) fresh bean sprouts
1 medium stalk celery, julienned
½ cup julienned cooked ham
½ cup julienned cooked chicken breast
5 green onions, cut into 1½-inch (4-cm) lengths

DRESSING
½ tsp finely chopped garlic
1 tsp red pepper flakes
½ tsp peppercorns, whole or freshly ground
1 tsp sugar
juice of 1 lemon (or lime)
1 cup mayonnaise
2 Tbsps fish soy (*nam pla*)

GARNISHES
2 Tbsps chopped fresh coriander leaves
1 Tbsp white sesame seeds, toasted (see page 11)

Pick over the bean sprouts—remove any black seed coverings and remove the roots if you are ambitious. Blanch them in boiling water for 1 minute. Drain and immediately plunge into cold water to stop the cooking process. Drain again.

Place the bean sprouts in a serving dish or salad bowl and arrange the celery, ham, chicken, and green onions attractively on top. Refrigerate.

In a mortar, pound the garlic, red pepper flakes, and peppercorns to a paste and add the sugar, lemon juice, fish soy, and mayonnaise. Blend well and refrigerate.

Just before serving, pour the DRESSING over the bean sprouts, ham, chicken, and green onion. Garnish with the coriander leaves and sesame seeds.

♠ Carrot and Shrimp Salad

This is a nice change from the more standard salads in eastern or western cooking. The dressing is sweet and sour—not at all spicy. Omit the chili pepper if you like.

SERVES 6–8

5 oz (150 gm) small or medium shrimp, shelled and deveined
10 oz (300 gm) carrots, scraped and finely shredded

DRESSING
1½ Tbsps All-Purpose Chili Sauce (see page 33)

⅓ cup coconut cream (substitute 3 Tbsps vegetable oil)

1 tsp sugar

2 Tbsps fish soy (*nam pla*)

juice of 1 lime

¼ cup peanuts, toasted in a dry frying pan briefly and coarsely chopped

1 head Boston lettuce

<small>GARNISHES</small>

10 cherry tomatoes, quartered

1 Tbsp chopped fresh coriander leaves (or 2 Tbsps chopped green onion)

Cook shrimp 1 minute in lightly salted boiling water. Cool and dice.

Mix the DRESSING ingredients.

Combine carrot, shrimp, and DRESSING and toss 5 minutes before serving.

Line a salad bowl with the lettuce and arrange the carrot and shrimp mixture on it. Garnish with the tomato quarters and fresh coriander (or green onion).

▲ Pork and Liver Salad
(color page 13)

The western cook would never think of cold pork or calf's liver as salad ingredients. This meat salad is almost a meal in itself and has a surprising and delightful flavor. The adventurous cook can add shrimp, chicken, squid, and saifun noodles and increase the amount of DRESSING accordingly. With these additions, this dish comes to resemble the famous Great Salad (Yam Yai).

SERVES 8

1 cup saké

2 tsps salt

11 oz (300 gm) pork shoulder

½ lb (250 gm) calf's (or pork) liver (not sliced)

1 head Boston lettuce

¼ lb (115 gm) bean sprouts, cleaned

1 cup julienned celery

1 cup julienned cucumber

1 cup julienned carrots

<small>DRESSING</small>

3–4 Tbsps fish soy (*nam pla*) or soy sauce

1 Tbsp sugar

2 Tbsps finely chopped garlic

3–4 Tbsps vegetable oil

1 Tbsp All-Purpose Chili Sauce (see page 33)

juice of 1 lemon

½ cup roughly chopped or crushed peanuts
2 Tbsps Chinese pickle (Tientsin Preserved Vegetable; optional)
2–3 Tbsps chopped fresh coriander leaves
4–5 red chili peppers, cut into fine slivers

Place 5 cups of water in a saucepan, add ½ cup saké, 1 tsp of salt, and the pork shoulder. Boil over medium heat until tender, about 30 minutes. Place 4 cups water and the remaining saké and salt in another saucepan, add the liver, and cook over medium heat about 20 minutes or until tender. Remove from the water and when cool enough to handle, slice both the pork and the liver into very thin (sukiyaki thin) slices and cut the slices into 1 × 2-inch (2 × 5-cm) pieces. Refrigerate.

Wash the lettuce and tear or cut it into 1-inch (2-cm) squares. Pour boiling water over the bean sprouts and let them stand for 1 minute. Drain and plunge into cold water. Combine the vegetables and refrigerate them.

Chop or crush the peanuts and chop the Chinese pickle slightly smaller than it already is.

Brown the 2 Tbsps garlic in the 3–4 Tbsps oil and reserve (garlic and oil).

Mix the DRESSING ingredients, including fried garlic and its oil, and put in a small bowl.

Line a shallow salad bowl or serving dish with the lettuce and decoratively arrange the vegetables, pork, and liver in mounds. Sprinkle with peanuts, Chinese pickle, coriander leaves, and chili pepper.

At the table, pour on DRESSING and toss immediately before eating.

♠ Tofu Chicken Salad

SERVES 8–10

1½ lbs (700 gm) regular tofu (Japanese "cotton" tofu)
1 cup cooked chicken white meat (leftover is fine) (vegetarians can
    substitute 1 cup button mushrooms)
½ cup coarsely julienned carrot
½ cup julienned celery
1 cup bean sprouts
3 green onions (with tops), cut into 2-inch (5-cm) lengths
2 Tbsps chopped fresh coriander leaves

DRESSING
1 Tbsp lemon juice
3 Tbsps fish soy (*nam pla*)
1 Tbsp All-Purpose Chili Sauce (see page 33)
4 Tbsps catsup
¾ cup mayonnaise
1 tsp sugar (optional)
2 Tbsps chopped fresh coriander leaves

Cut the tofu into ¼ × ¼ × 1½-inch (1 × 1 × 4-cm) pieces. Place in a colander and let drain for 20 minutes.

Tear the chicken into pencil-sized shreds.

In a shallow salad bowl or serving dish arrange the salad ingredients in concentric circles of alternating colors: first the tofu around the rim, then the julienned carrot, the celery, the bean sprouts, and finally the shredded chicken in the center.

Sprinkle the coriander and green onions over everything before refrigerating for at least 30 minutes.

Blend all DRESSING ingredients and chill.

Pour the DRESSING over the salad and toss it gently just before serving.

♣ Cucumber Salad
(Yam Dang)

This piquant and interesting salad, featuring the flavor of young ginger, takes a little time to prepare, but it is worth it. Young ginger is in season from spring to autumn and has plump rhizomes with ivory-white skin.

SERVES 6

DRESSING

3 dried red chili peppers, seeded, soaked in water for 5 minutes
  (substitute 2 tsps cayenne pepper)
½ tsp peppercorns, whole or freshly ground
2 tsps coarsely chopped garlic
2 Tbsps fish soy (nam pla)
1 tsp sugar
3 Tbsps vegetable oil
juice of ½ lemon (or lime)

½ lb (225 gm) cucumbers, peeled, seeded and cut into ¼ × ¼ × 2-inch
  (¾ × ¾ × 5-cm) strips
2 oz (60 gm) young ginger shoots (optional; substitute 2 green onions),
  cut into very fine slivers
2 oz (60 gm) celery, julienned
½ cup dried shrimp, rinsed

GARNISH

1 Tbsp chopped fresh coriander leaves

Pound or blend the dried chilies, peppercorns, and garlic to a paste. Mix in the fish soy, sugar, oil, and lemon (or lime) juice. Combine the vegetables and dried shrimp. Add the DRESSING and toss.

Place in a salad bowl and sprinkle with coriander leaves.

Note: You can sometimes find bottled ginger shoots or sliced or shredded sweet vinegared ginger in oriental food stores. These may be used in place of the fresh young ginger shoots.

♠ Cucumber Pickles

Instant cucumber pickles such as these two are found throughout the countries of Southeast Asia. They accompany grilled meats and fried foods, serving to counteract oily flavors as well as to enhance the flavor of fish and poultry dishes.

Japanese cucumbers are preferred for these two recipes. The thick-skinned western cucumber should be peeled and seeded before using.

PICKLE A

SERVES 6–8

3 cups thinly sliced cucumbers
⅓ cup coarsely chopped onion
½ cup red or white wine vinegar
2 tsps sugar
¼ tsp salt
3–4 fresh red chili peppers, seeded
1 Tbsp fresh coriander leaves

Combine all ingredients and serve.

PICKLE B

SERVES 6–8

3 cups thinly sliced cucumbers
½ small onion, thinly sliced

A MIXTURE
2 dried red chili peppers, seeded (or 1 tsp cayenne pepper)
2 tsps chopped garlic
2 tsps chopped coriander root
2 tsps peppercorns, whole or freshly ground

B MIXTURE
½ cup vinegar
2 Tbsps fish soy (*nam pla*)
1½ tsps sugar
1 Tbsp chopped fresh coriander leaves
½ cup crushed peanuts

Place cucumber and onion in a bowl and toss.

Place the A MIXTURE in a blender or food processor and whir to make a rough paste (or pound in a mortar). Blend the B MIXTURE, then mix together A and B. Immediately pour over the cucumbers and sliced onion.

Place in a serving dish and sprinkle with coriander leaves and crushed peanuts. Serve immediately.

You may wish to add more chilies or cayenne pepper if you like it hot.

▲ Mushroom Salad
(Yam Hed)

SERVES 6–8

5 oz (150 gm) sliced smoked salmon (or fresh shrimp)
10 oz (300 gm) button mushrooms, thinly sliced
½ cup mint leaves, torn into small pieces

SEASONINGS
½ tsp salt
1 tsp finely chopped garlic
1 tsp red pepper flakes
juice of ½ lemon or lime
2 Tbsps fish soy (nam pla)
½ tsp sugar
2 Tbsps vegetable oil

¼ cup thinly sliced red onion

Cut the salmon into 1-inch (2-cm) squares. (If using shrimp rather than salmon, shell, devein, and boil briefly in salted water.)

After slicing the mushrooms (use the stems if they are tender), put them into lightly salted water for 2–3 minutes to keep them white. Toss the drained mushrooms, smoked salmon, and mint and refrigerate.

Pound the salt, garlic, and red pepper flakes in a mortar and mix with remaining SEASONINGS ingredients. Pour this over the mushrooms, salmon, and mint just before serving and sprinkle with the sliced red onion. (Red onions look nice, but any kind of onion will do.)

▲ Saifun Noodle Salad
(Yam Woon Sen)

This easy-to-make salad travels to picnics or pot-luck affairs very well.

SERVES 6–8

¼ lb (115 gm) saifun noodles (Chinese type preferred; Japanese harusame gets mushy)
½ lb (225 gm) ground pork
⅓ cup dried shrimp, rinsed and well pounded in a mortar

DRESSING
½ cup peanuts, coarsely chopped or crushed

2 Tbsps finely chopped green onion

3 Tbsps fish soy (*nam pla*)

juice of 1 lemon

1 Tbsp sugar

1½ tsps red pepper flakes

2 Tbsps vegetable oil

2 large heads Boston lettuce

GARNISH

1 Tbsp chopped fresh coriander leaves or finely chopped green onion

Place saifun noodles in a bowl, pour on boiling water to cover, and soak for 15–20 minutes. Drain and rinse in cold water. Drain again.

Stir-fry the pork over medium heat until it turns white. Cool. Mix the noodles, pork, and shrimp.

Blend the DRESSING ingredients and add to the noodle mixture. Arrange the lettuce leaves in a circle on a serving plate. Put the noodle mixture in the middle and sprinkle with chopped coriander leaves or green onion before serving.

Note: If you like a very strong shrimp flavor, do not rinse the dried shrimp.

♠ Thai Tuna Salad
(*Yam Pra Gabong*)

This is a widely popular dish in Thailand, easy to prepare, and un-complicated—home cooking.

SERVES 6–8

½ lb (225 gm) fresh tuna or sea bass fillets (substitute 1 6-oz can tuna)

¼ lb (115 gm) cabbage, cut into ½ × 1½-inch (1 × 4-cm) pieces

3 green onions, finely chopped

½ tsp fresh lemon grass, finely chopped (or 1 tsp dried)

lettuce or young spinach

DRESSING

3 Tbsps rice vinegar

1 tsp sugar

1 Tbsp All-Purpose Chili Sauce (see page 33)

2 Tbsps fish soy (*nam pla*)

2 Tbsps vegetable oil

GARNISH

1 Tbsp chopped fresh coriander leaves

If using fresh fish fillets, broil them until just done, cool, then flake. (If using canned tuna, drain and flake it.) Add the cabbage, onions, and lemon grass to the flaked fish. Mix and refrigerate.

Mix the DRESSING ingredients and add to the fish about 10 minutes before serving.

Line a salad bowl with lettuce or young spinach leaves. Arrange the marinated fish on this, then sprinkle with coriander leaves.

This would be more authentically Thai if it was hotter. You can add chilies or chili paste. If you can get them, the fiercely hot, tiny Thai chilies known as *prik kee nu* are excellent sprinkled over this salad. Any very hot Mexican chilies, chopped, would be a good substitute.

▲ Eggplant Salad

Even people who do not care for eggplant will like this. The flavors are uncomplicated, and it is simple to prepare.

SERVES 6

8 medium Japanese eggplants (2 medium western eggplants)

1 tsp finely chopped coriander root
½ tsp peppercorns, whole or freshly ground
1 Tbsp finely chopped garlic

SEASONINGS

1 tsp sugar
2 Tbsps fish soy (*nam pla*)
2 tsps regular chili powder (the Mexican type)
2 Tbsps vegetable oil
juice of ½ lemon (or lime)

GARNISHES

2 green onions, finely chopped
⅔ oz (20 gm) dried bonito flakes (Japanese *katsuo-bushi*) or
    ½ cup dried shrimp, rinsed and lightly pounded

Peel the eggplants and cut them into ¼ × ¼ × 2-inch (¾ × ¾ × 5-cm) strips. Steam the eggplant strips for 10 minutes. (You could boil the eggplant, but it will lose flavor.) Set aside to cool.

Pound the coriander root, peppercorns, and garlic to a paste in a mortar and add the SEASONINGS to make a sauce. Toss the cooked eggplant with the sauce and let sit for 15 minutes.

Place the marinated eggplant in a serving dish and sprinkle with the dried bonito flakes (or dried shrimp) and the chopped green onion. Serve at room temperature.

♠ Three-Color Seafood Salad

(color page 15)

The contrast of the snow-white squid on its bed of green lettuce with the ebony or ruby red cavier makes this an eye-appealing addition to any meal.

SERVES 6–8

DRESSING

½ Tbsp ground red pepper
½ Tbsp finely chopped garlic
1 tsp sugar (optional)
2½ Tbsps fish soy (*nam pla*)
juice of ½ lemon
3 Tbsps vegetable oil

1 lb (450 gm) raw squid
1 medium head Boston lettuce
1 small jar red (or black) lumpfish caviar
¼ cup julienned green onion
½ Tbsp chopped fresh coriander leaves
½ tsp finely chopped fresh lemon grass (optional)

Pound the red pepper, garlic, and sugar to a paste with a mortar and pestle. Add the remaining DRESSING ingredients and blend them thoroughly.

Use only the squid body. (Reserve tentacles for some other use.) Clean well, slit open to form a flat sheet, and remove the thin, speckled skin. Place the flat sheet of squid with the skin side down and score it lightly at ¼-inch (¾-cm) intervals. Score again at a diagonal to the first, to form a diamond pattern. Cut into 1 × 1½-inch (2 × 4-cm) pieces. Parboil the squid for 1 minute in lightly salted boiling water. Plunge immediately into cold water to stop the cooking process. Drain. (Squid is tender with very short or long cooking times; otherwise it is rubber.)

Place the well-washed lettuce in a circle around the edge of a serving dish. Place the squid in a ring closer to the center and finally put the caviar in the center of the plate. Sprinkle the green onion, the chopped coriander leaves, and the lemon grass over the salad.

Refrigerate both the salad and the DRESSING. Just before serving, pour the DRESSING over the salad.

♠ Mixed Meat Salad

(*Lab Nya*)

This is an extravagant salad and may be eaten with the fingers. Diners tear off a piece of lettuce, place some mixed meats on the leaf, roll it up, and. . . . Messy. Delicious.

1⅔ lbs (800 gm) lean beef (rump steak or Swiss steak works well)

5 oz (150 gm) calf's liver

5 oz (150 gm) tripe

1½ Tbsps finely grated or chopped garlic

2 Tbsps red wine (or saké)

½ cup parched rice (see page 119)

1½ Tbsps finely chopped fresh (or 1 Tbsp dried) lemon grass

3 green onions, chopped

2 Tbsps chopped fresh coriander leaves

½ cup fresh mint leaves, roughly torn

6 shallots (substitute red onion), thinly sliced

DRESSING

2 Tbsps Thai salt-preserved fish (*pla la*; substitute anchovy paste)

1–2 Tbsps fish soy (*nam pla*)

½ cup lemon juice

½–1 Tbsp crushed or chopped guinea peppers (*prik kee nu*)

2 green onions, chopped

1 large head Boston lettuce

Wash the beef and chop it coarsely—like a fine dice. (Take care if using a food processor—hamburger is much too fine for this dish.) Add the chopped beef to an ample amount of boiling water and cook it only 1 minute. The meat will still be pink. Drain the beef and set it aside.

Cook the piece of calf's liver in boiling water over medium heat to cover for about 15 minutes. Remove, cool, and slice. Cut the sliced liver into ½ × 1½-inch (1 × 4-cm) pieces.

Wash the tripe and boil in ample water over medium heat for about 15 minutes or until tender. Slice and cut into ¼ × 1½-inch (¾ × 4-cm) pieces.

Mix garlic and wine (or saké). Marinate all three meats separately in this mixture for 5 minutes.

Mix all the DRESSING ingredients.

There are two ways to serve the salad. One is to place the mixed meats on lettuce leaves and garnish with parched rice, lemon grass, green onion, mint, and shallots. Toss at the table, then pour on the DRESSING.

An easier way is to toss the meats and all other ingredients, including the DRESSING, then place on lettuce leaves.

As described above, diners tear off a piece of lettuce, place morsels of different meats on the lettuce, roll, and enjoy.

Pla la (Thai salt-preserved fish): Pour 3 Tbsps boiling water over the *pla la*. Dissolve it and strain out the fish bones and bits of fish scales. If using anchovy paste, simply dissolve 2 Tbsps paste in 3 Tbsps boiling water.

♠Thai Tenderloin Salad

Meat salads are very Thai, but this is an original, not a classic salad. In Thailand, the hotter the meat salad, the better. It makes Thai beer taste good.

Clearly this is a meal in itself, and it is a snap to prepare. What more does one need?

SERVES 6–8

1 lb (450 gm) beef tenderloin, very thinly sliced (sukiyaki style)

½ cup coarsely chopped fresh mint leaves

¼ cup finely shredded shallots (substitute red onion)

2 green onions, coarsely chopped

DRESSING

juice of 1 lime (or ½ lemon)

2 Tbsps fish soy (*nam pla*)

½ tsp cayenne pepper

1 Tbsp All-Purpose Chili Sauce (see page 33)

1 tsp sugar

GARNISHES

5–7 guinea peppers (*prik kee nu*), coarsely chopped

1 Tbsp chopped fresh coriander leaves

2 Tbsps parched long-grain rice (see page 119; substitute Grape Nuts)

Cut the sliced beef into 2 × 3-inch (5 × 8-cm) pieces. Place the meat in a slotted spoon or small colander and dip it into boiling water for 1 minute (it should be medium rare). Allow the meat to drain and cool while combining the DRESSING ingredients. You can also use cold leftover roast beef sliced very thin.

Arrange the beef in a salad bowl, sprinkle with the fresh mint leaves, shallots, and green onion. Add the DRESSING and refrigerate until ready to serve.

Sprinkle the parched rice, the coriander leaves, and the chopped guinea peppers over the salad just before serving. Toss at the table.

♠Marinated Green Beans and Shrimp

In any place with good, fresh green beans, this salad becomes something marvelous. It can be prepared half a day ahead.

SERVES 6–8

1 lb (450 gm) green beans

2 lemon wedges

pinch of salt

½ lb (225 gm) fresh medium shrimp, shelled and deveined

2 Tbsps Roasted Chili Sauce (see page 38)
juice of 1 lemon
½ tsp sugar (optional)
1 tsp red pepper flakes (optional)
2–2½ Tbsps fish soy (*nam pla*)

GARNISHES

2 green onions, cut into 1½-inch (4-cm) lengths
2 Tbsps garlic oil (see page 10)

Cut the green beans on a sharp diagonal into 1½-inch (4-cm) lengths. Bring 4 cups of water to a boil, add the beans, turn the heat off, and leave them for 1 minute. Plunge them immediately into cold water and drain.

Bring 2 cups of water to a boil. Add the lemon wedges, salt, and shrimp. Turn off the heat and let the shrimp sit only 1 minute. Plunge immediately into cold water and drain.

Mix the beans and shrimp, then blend the DRESSING ingredients, pour the DRESSING on the beans and shrimp, and mix again.

Add the green onion and the garlic oil to the beans and shrimp. Refrigerate at least 30 minutes to allow the flavors to blend.

♠ Spicy Tofu Salad
(color page 13)

This salad has an unusual combination of flavors and is a full meal in itself—for lunch or a summer dinner. Good with chilled white wine and brioche.

SERVES 8–10

1½ lbs (700 gm) regular tofu (Japanese "cotton" tofu)
1 cup julienned cucumber
1 cup julienned carrot
1 cup sliced button mushrooms
½ lb (225 gm) fresh shrimp, shelled, deveined, and blanched
1 small head iceberg lettuce

TOPPING

⅓ cup dried shrimp, rinsed and lightly pounded in a mortar
2 green onions, coarsely chopped
5–6 mixed red and green chili peppers, coarsely chopped

DRESSING

1–1½ Tbsps Roasted Chili Sauce (see page 38)
3 Tbsps fish soy (*nam pla*)
2 tsps sugar
½ cup rice (or cider) vinegar
½ cup mayonnaise

Cut the tofu into ¼ × 1 × 1½-inch (¾ × 2 × 4-cm) pieces. Drain it in a colander.

Put the lettuce on the bottom of a shallow bowl or attractive serving dish. Place tofu in the center and surround it with one mound each of cucumber, carrot, mushroom, and shrimp. Refrigerate until chilled.

Combine the TOPPING ingredients in a blender or food processor and whir to form a rough mixture (or pound in a mortar).

Blend DRESSING ingredients.

At serving time sprinkle the TOPPING mixture over the salad, then pour on the DRESSING and toss it at the table.

Variation
For the vegetarian, shrimp can be replaced by lightly cooked lima beans, and peanuts or sunflower seeds (practically any nuts will do) can take the place of dried shrimp in the TOPPING.

♠ Quail Eggs with Tomatoes

Here is a good example of a western idea given energy and punch with Thai flavors.

SERVES 6–8

15 fresh quail eggs (substitute 5 small chicken eggs), hard-boiled and peeled

2 Japanese cucumbers, peeled (or 1 western cucumber, peeled and seeded)

¼ cup thinly sliced onion

½ stalk celery, stringed

½ lb (225 gm) cherry tomatoes

1 cup seeded black olives

DRESSING

3–4 coriander roots, crushed

3–4 peppercorns, whole or freshly ground

½ tsp salt

1 Tbsp fish soy (*nam pla*)

1–2 tsps sugar

1–2 tsps cayenne pepper

juice of ½ lime (or lemon)

3–4 Tbsps vegetable oil

GARNISHES

2 green onions, chopped

2 fresh red chili peppers, cut lengthwise into fine slivers

Cut the eggs in half crosswise (not through the poles).

Cut the cucumbers into ½ × 1 × 1-inch (1 × 2 × 2-cm) pieces. Cut the thin onion slices in half. Cut the celery into ½-inch (1-cm) chunks. Mix the eggs and vegetables, place on a serving dish, and refrigerate for 30 minutes.

Meanwhile prepare the DRESSING. Do not use a blender for this—it needs a coarse texture. Pound the coriander roots and peppercorns in a mortar. Combine these with all other DRESSING ingredients and shake in a jar. Keep at room temperature until ready to serve.

Just before serving, pour the DRESSING on the vegetables, then sprinkle with green onion and red chili.

Variation

If you would like to use this as an interesting vegetable dish with a western meal it is probably wise to omit the chili and fish soy, since they have such strong characteristics. Use anchovy paste in place of the fish soy and just leave out the powdered red pepper (and fresh red chilies, too, if you like).

▲ Green Papaya Salad
(*Som Tom*)

SERVES 6

DRESSING

2 tsps chopped garlic

2–3 fresh or dried red chili peppers, seeded, (soaked), and coarsely chopped

1 Tbsp sugar

2 Tbsps fish soy (*nam pla*)

juice of 1 lemon

3 cups coarsely grated or julienned hard, green papaya (do not use those beginning to ripen)

½ lb (225 gm) green beans, julienned

½ cup dried shrimp, rinsed and lightly pounded

GARNISHES

¼ lb (115 gm) cherry tomatoes, quartered

4 Tbsps coarsely chopped or crushed peanuts

raw cabbage leaves, torn into bite-sized chunks

In a mortar, pound the garlic, chilies, and sugar to a paste, then mix in the fish soy and lemon juice.

Mix the papaya, green beans, and shrimp and refrigerate until ready to serve.

At serving time, pour on the DRESSING and sprinkle the peanuts and cherry tomatoes over the papaya mixture. Serve with chunks of raw cabbage leaves and enjoy a cacophony of flavors.

VEGETABLES

ผัก

Although the pragmatic Thai Buddhists do eat meat, vegetables play an important role in the Thai diet. Food is abundant, so the keynote is variety. Many of the familiar European vegetables are used, and there is a host of decidedly exotic, local ones. Some of the familiar vegetables, like celery and kohlrabi, are fairly recent additions to the Thai diet. The fact that most of the more exotic vegetables are not available fresh outside of Southeast Asia is unfortunate, but, as with ingredients of other once exotic and now familiar cuisines, some day this will be corrected, as Thai cooking becomes more popular (and some enterprising farmers in Florida or California take a few risks).

The variety of vegetables in Thailand is enormous, but the methods of preparing and serving them is surprisingly limited. Perhaps the most common is eating vegetables raw, which means that they must be of the highest quality—tender and succulent. Raw vegetables might be dipped into various sauces (found in the Chili Sauces section, pages 33-39) or used in salads. The latter are always served on mounds of crisp lettuce and are garnished with the ubiquitous coriander leaves. Vegetables are also stir-fried and lightly steamed.

Mention must be made of the fantastic carved vegetables used in special dishes and for special occasions. The carving and cutting of these spectacular garnishes is a highly developed art unsurpassed anywhere in the world (including Japan).

♠ Stir-Fried Greens with Oyster Sauce

SERVES 6

½ lb (225 gm) greens (collard greens, mustard greens, bok choy, or even broccoli)

3 Tbsps vegetable oil

1 Tbsp finely chopped garlic

SEASONINGS

1 Tbsp fish soy (*nam pla*)

1 Tbsp bean paste (Chinese or Japanese; either white or red)

2 Tbsps oyster sauce

1 Tbsp cornstarch dissolved in ¼ cup water

GARNISH

1 Tbsp chopped fresh coriander leaves

Wash the vegetables. Cut leafy greens into 2-inch (5-cm) lengths (or separate the broccoli into ¼-inch/¾-cm florets; peel and cut the stem into thin slices). Heat the oil in a wok over high heat and add the garlic. Stir-fry until it is light brown, then add the greens and SEASONINGS (including cornstarch-water mixture). Stir-fry for 3–5 minutes more. Transfer to a serving dish, sprinkle with coriander leaves, and serve hot.

♠ Stuffed Peppers—Thai Style
(*Prik Yat Sai*)
(color page 16)

SERVES 6–8

8 small green peppers

FILLING

½ lb (225 gm) ground pork (vegetarians can substitute an
    equal amount of chopped fresh mushrooms)

2 oz (60 gm) raw shrimp, shelled, deveined, and coarsely chopped

2 Tbsps chopped green onion

1 Tbsp chopped garlic

½ tsp chopped fresh ginger

¼ tsp pepper

¼ tsp sugar (optional)

½ Tbsp cornstarch dissolved in 1 Tbsp water

GARNISHES

vegetable oil

2 dried red chili peppers, seeded and cut into fine slivers

Cut the tops off the green peppers, seed them, and set them aside. Mix the FILLING ingredients thoroughly and stuff the peppers. Place them in a flat baking dish and bake them in a preheated 350° F/175° C oven for 30 minutes. In Thailand, where ovens are still rare, these are steamed over high heat for 30 minutes.

Before serving, brush the peppers with oil to make them shine and sprinkle them with slivers of dried bright red chili peppers. Serve the stuffed peppers hot or at room temperature with the following tomato sauce.

TOMATO SAUCE
½ cup canned tomato sauce
1 Tbsp All-Purpose Chili Sauce (see page 33)
1 Tbsp lemon juice

Mix and serve with stuffed peppers.

♨ Stir-Fried Bean Sprouts with Tofu

SERVES 6–8

12 oz (360 gm) regular tofu (Japanese ''cotton'' tofu)
4 Tbsps vegetable oil
1 Tbsp finely chopped garlic
5 oz (150 gm) sliced pork, cut into julienne strips
1 lb (450 gm) bean sprouts
5 green onions, cut into 1½-inch (4-cm) lengths
pinch salt
⅓ tsp black pepper
2 Tbsps fish soy (_nam pla_)

Drain the tofu for 10 minutes, then cut it into ½ × ½ × 1-inch (1 × 1 × 2-cm) pieces. Add 2 Tbsps oil to a wok or frying pan over medium heat and stir-fry the garlic in the hot oil until it turns golden. Set aside.

Add the pork and stir-fry for 2–3 minutes. Add the remaining 2 Tbsps oil and let it get hot, then add the tofu to the pan. Stir-fry an additional 5 minutes. Add the bean sprouts, chopped green onions, salt, pepper, fish soy, and the reserved garlic oil. Stir-fry only 1 minute. Just before serving, sprinkle an additional dash of black pepper over the mixture. Serve hot.

♨ Stir-Fried Asparagus with Mushrooms

Although definitely oriental in flavor, this lends itself to many western meals, especially roasts.

SERVES 6–8

½ lb (225 gm) fresh asparagus
1 beef bouillon cube
1 Tbsp cornstarch

4 Tbsps vegetable oil
1 Tbsp chopped garlic
6 fresh shiitake mushrooms, stems removed and each cut into 3–4 slices
2 green onions (tops included), cut into 1½-inch (4-cm) lengths
1½ Tbsps oyster sauce
freshly ground black pepper

Clean the asparagus and trim off the tough stalk bottoms. Parboil for 2–3 minutes (it may take longer with very thick asparagus).

Dissolve the bouillon cube in ½ cup water, then add the cornstarch and stir to dissolve.

Put the oil in a wok or frying pan over medium-high heat and heat almost to the smoking point. Add the chopped garlic and brown it before adding the asparagus, mushrooms, and green onions all at once. Immediately add the oyster sauce and bouillon with cornstarch. Stir-fry over medium-high heat for 3 minutes, during which time the sauce will thicken.

Place in a serving dish and grind black pepper over to taste.

Frozen asparagus can be substituted for fresh asparagus and even canned asparagus can be used, but the result will be quite different, since canned asparagus is so soft.

♨ Potatoes in Coconut Milk

This is a kind of gratin.

SERVES 6–8

2 lbs (1 kg) potatoes
3 Tbsps vegetable oil
1½ Tbsps crushed garlic
½ cup flour mixed into ½ cup water
2 cups coconut milk
white pepper
salt
2 Tbsps white or black sesame seeds

Peel the potatoes and slice them into thick rounds. Boil them until they are almost half done (about 10 minutes). Drain and set aside.

Heat the oil in a frying pan over medium heat and brown the garlic. Add the flour-water mixture to the garlic with the 2 cups of coconut milk. Continue to cook and stir until thickened. Season the "coconut white sauce" with pepper and salt. If it seems thicker than a conventional white sauce, add a little water to thin it down.

Add the potatoes and stir until they are thoroughly coated. Put the potatoes and sauce in a casserole and sprinkle with sesame seeds. Bake in a moderate oven (350° F/175° C) for 30 minutes or until lightly browned.

Good sprinkled with browned onion bits before serving.

♠ Braised Vegetables

This recipe is a great vegetable drawer tidier. Use whatever fresh vegetable orphans or remnants you have in the house.

SERVES 6–8

1 medium carrot
1½-inch (4-cm) length daikon radish (substitute icicle radish)
¼ lb (115 gm) fresh mushrooms (any kind)
5 oz (150 gm) winter melon (substitute yellow squash)
1 green pepper

6-8 cups weak chicken (or vegetable) stock (see page 11)

4 Tbsps vegetable oil
1 tsp finely chopped fresh ginger
½ lb (225 gm) ground meat (substitute 2 Tbsps any *miso*)
1½ Tbsps cornstarch
1 cup water left from boiling the vegetables
½ tsp salt
½ tsp pepper
1 Tbsp fish soy (*nam pla*)

GARNISH
1 green onion, chopped

Cut all vegetables into ½ × ½ × 1-inch (1 × 1 × 2-cm) pieces.

Put the chicken stock in a large saucepan. Add the first 4 vegetables (not the quick-cooking green pepper), bring to a boil, and cook over medium heat for 15 minutes. Add the green pepper during the last 2 minutes of cooking. Drain the vegetables and save the cooking water.

Place the oil in a wok over high heat. When very hot, add the ginger and meat and stir-fry for 3 minutes, until the meat is cooked.

Dissolve the cornstarch in 1 cup of the leftover vegetable stock and add it to the wok with the salt, pepper, fish soy, and boiled vegetables. Cook, stirring constantly, for 3–5 minutes or until the liquid thickens. Place in a serving dish and sprinkle with chopped green onion before serving.

Double-Duty Soup
Place the remaining vegetable stock back over medium heat and bring to a boil. Very lightly beat 2 eggs, adding salt and pepper to taste. Add the beaten eggs when the stock is gently boiling. Sprinkle some chopped green onion and chopped coriander leaves into the soup pot, and you will have a simple but tasty soup.

♠ Green Beans with Crab

In Thailand very long beans (up to 2 feet long) are used. They are very similar in taste and texture to the pole beans found in American gardens. Unlike some Thai vegetable dishes, this one is rather thick—not juicy.

¼ lb (115 gm) fresh (or 2 oz/60 gm dried) shiitake mushrooms
4 Tbsps vegetable oil
1 Tbsp finely chopped garlic
½ lb (225 gm) green beans, cut diagonally into 1½-inch (4-cm) pieces
2 green onions, cut into 1½-inch (4-cm) lengths
¼ lb (115 gm) cooked or canned crab, cartilage removed

SEASONINGS
2 Tbsps fish soy (*nam pla*) or regular soy sauce
½ tsp black pepper
1 Tbsp cornstarch mixed with 2 Tbsps water

GARNISH
1 Tbsp chopped fresh coriander leaves

If using dried shiitake mushrooms, reconstitute in warm water to cover for 30 minutes. Drain. With both reconstituted and fresh mushrooms, trim off stems and cut caps into medium-sized slices.

Put the oil in a wok and stir-fry the garlic over high heat just until it begins to brown. Add the mushrooms and stir-fry for 1–2 minutes. Add the green beans and stir-fry for 1–2 minutes. Add the green onion, crab, and the SEASONINGS at the same time. Immediately add ¼ cup cold water. Continue to stir-fry for 2–3 minutes, until the liquid thickens. Place in a serving dish and sprinkle with chopped coriander leaves.

Variation
Substitute the same amount of cooked shrimp for the crab.

⚜ Sautéed Winter Squash with Bacon

The Asian "winter squash" (which ripens in late summer and early autumn) resembles a small pumpkin with (usually) green skin. Some of the Japanese varieties of squash, known generically as kabocha, are becoming available in North America. Besides their fine flavor and convenient shape, the skin of these squash or pumpkins cooks easily and can be eaten. If you use a tougher-skinned variety of winter squash, such as butternut or acorn, peel it first.

SERVES 6–8

2 Tbsps finely chopped onion
¼ lb (115 gm) sliced bacon (about 5 slices), cut into julienne strips
2–3 Tbsps vegetable oil
½ cup dried shrimp, rinsed
1 lb (450 gm) winter squash, cut into large julienne strips

SEASONINGS
1 Tbsp fish soy (*nam pla*)
½ tsp salt

½ tsp pepper
1 Tbsp honey

Put the onion and bacon in a wok or frying pan over medium heat and cook until the bacon fat is rendered. Remove the bacon fat. Add the vegetable oil and dried shrimp and stir-fry 30 seconds or so. Add the squash. Stir and add the SEASONINGS and 3–4 Tbsps water. Cover and cook for 20 minutes, until squash is tender but not too soft. Serve hot.

▲ Stir-Fried Sweet-and-Sour Vegetables
(*Pat Pak Priaw Wan*)
(color page 15)

SERVES 8–10

3 cucumbers (Japanese if possible)
3 medium underripe tomatoes
1 medium onion
3 green peppers, seeded
2 fresh red chili peppers
½ cup vegetable oil
3 cloves garlic, crushed
1 lb (450 gm) fresh medium shrimp, shelled and deveined

SEASONINGS
1½ Tbsps cornstarch dissolved in 1 cup water
2–2½ Tbsps fish soy (*nam pla*)
½ tsp pepper
1 Tbsp sugar
1½–2 Tbsps vinegar

GARNISH
3 green onions, cut into 1½-inch (4-cm) lengths or 1 Tbsp fresh
    chopped coriander leaves

Wash but do not peel the cucumbers. Cut them lengthwise into quarters and then crosswise into 3–4 pieces. (If using western cucumbers, seed them.) Cut the tomatoes and the onion into eighths.

Cut the green peppers into 2-inch (5-cm) pieces. Seed the chili peppers and cut each lengthwise into 4–5 pieces.

Put the ½ cup of oil in a wok, heat it over medium-high heat, add the 3 cloves of garlic, and fry them until they turn light brown. Add the shrimp and stir-fry over high heat for 1–2 minutes. Remove shrimp and garlic.

Add all other vegetables and stir-fry over high heat for 2–3 minutes. Dissolve the cornstarch in the water and add it with all the SEASONINGS. Stir until sauce thickens. Adjust for seasoning—the flavor should be sweet, sour, and salty all at once. Return the shrimp and garlic to the pan and warm.

Place in a serving dish and garnish with green onion or coriander leaves.

♠ Snow Peas with Scallops
(color page 17)

SERVES 6

4 Tbsps vegetable oil

2 cloves garlic, crushed

5 oz (150 gm) scallops, sliced into ¼-inch (¾-cm) thick rounds

3 cups snow peas, stringed

½ tsp black pepper

1 Tbsp not too salty bean paste (Chinese or Japanese)

1 Tbsp cornstarch dissolved in ¼ cup water

GARNISH

2 green onions, cut into 1½-inch (4-cm) lengths

Put the vegetable oil in a wok or frying pan over medium-high heat. Add the garlic and stir-fry just until it begins to turn light brown. Add the scallops and stir-fry 1–2 minutes. Remove the scallops and garlic but leave the oil in the wok.

Add the snow peas and stir-fry 2–3 minutes. Add the black pepper, bean paste, and cornstarch dissolved in water. Stir-fry 2 additional minutes, return the scallops and garlic to the pan, and cook until warmed. Place in a serving dish and sprinkle with green onion. Serve hot.

♠ Winter Squash in Coconut Milk

Slightly sweet and very coconutty, this is good as an accompaniment to curries or as a side dish for any meal.

SERVES 6–8

2 lbs (1 kg) winter squash (see comment, page 89)

3 cups coconut milk

½ cup dried shrimp, rinsed and coarsely pounded in a mortar

1 tsp peppercorns, whole or freshly ground

2 Tbsps chopped shallots (substitute red onion)

1 tsp shrimp paste (*kapi*)

5 oz (150 gm) medium shrimp, shelled and deveined

3 Tbsps fish soy (*nam pla*)

1 tsp sugar (or to taste)

Peel the winter squash and cut it into 1-inch (2-cm) chunks. Place the coconut milk in a saucepan over medium heat. Add the dried shrimp, peppercorns, chopped shallots, and shrimp paste. When the mixture boils, add the squash. Cook for 15 minutes (squash should be tender but not mushy) and add the shrimp. Cook 5 more minutes and add the fish soy and sugar. Bring just to a boil, remove from heat, and serve.

▲ Whole Stuffed Cabbage
(*Nung Gra Lampii*)

SERVES 8

1 large cabbage
½ lb (225 gm) ground pork (or ground chicken breast)
¼ lb (115 gm) fresh or canned crab meat, cartilage removed
¼ lb (115 gm) fresh shrimp, shelled and deveined (or use cooked shrimp)
3 egg yolks, beaten

SEASONINGS
5 peppercorns, whole or freshly ground
¼ tsp salt
1 tsp coarsely chopped coriander root
1 Tbsp coarsely chopped garlic
3 Tbsps fish soy (*nam pla*)

Select a large head of cabbage. Remove the tough, outer dark-green leaves.

Mix the pork (or chicken), crab, shrimp, and egg yolks. In a blender, food processor, or mortar, make a rough paste of the SEASONINGS and mix well with the meat-seafood mixture.

Remove the hard core, then steam the cabbage head briefly—just enough to soften the leaves.

Working with the whole cabbage, gently spread the outer leaves apart. Be careful not to break them off from the head. Distribute the meat-seafood mixture as evenly as possible throughout the whole cabbage—you probably will not be able to reach the center leaves.

Place the entire cabbage in a steamer and steam for 45 minutes or until the cabbage is tender. Remove to a serving plate and cut the cabbage into 6 or 8 wedges at the table.

▲ Gang Ba Curry with Straw Mushrooms
(*Gang Ba Hed*)

This is only one form of the very common gang ba *dishes. You can use any vegetables you have on hand, such as eggplant, zucchini, fresh or frozen corn, cauliflower, or bamboo shoots. Gang ba* curry paste lends itself *especially well to vegetarian curries.*

SERVES 4–6

4 hard-boiled eggs
10 oz (300 gm) fresh straw mushrooms (substitute oyster mushrooms or button mushrooms)
¼ cup vegetable oil
2–2½ Tbsps *Gang Ba* Curry Paste (page 27)
1½–2 Tbsps fish soy (*nam pla*)
½ tsp sugar (optional)

½ cup fresh holy basil (*bai krapau*) (or 3½ Tbsps dried, soaked
in ½ cup water 5 minutes)
2 fresh (or dried) kaffir lime leaves (*bai makrut*), torn roughly
6–7 fresh red chili peppers, cut lengthwise into 4–5 pieces

Peel the boiled eggs and cut them in half. Clean the fresh straw mushrooms, and, if they are very large, cut them in half lengthwise.

Put the ¼ cup vegetable oil in a wok or frying pan over medium heat. Add the curry paste and stir-fry until it releases its aroma—a few seconds only. Add the eggs and cook for 1 minute. Add 3 cups of water, the mushrooms, fish soy, and sugar (if using). Bring to a boil, still over medium heat. Adjust the seasoning to taste. Add the holy basil, kaffir lime leaves, and chili peppers. Mix gently. Remove from heat and serve hot with rice.

EGGS, TOFU

ไข่ — เต้าหู้

In the past, duck eggs were more common than chicken eggs, but today both are eaten throughout Thailand. The Salted Eggs recipe on page 97 was originally for duck eggs.

A beaten egg, quickly stir-fried in hot oil, often appears in a Thai meal. The Thai Omelette (page 98) is a staple in many restaurants. And always among the gleaming pots of the day's curries in Thai curry shops, one will find a large pot of Egg Stew (page 98). Several Thai curries use eggs as the main ingredients. Or, as with Son-in-Law Eggs (page 97), an egg dish is eaten as an accompaniment and complement to a hot curry.

The tofu most familiar in the West is the Japanese or Korean variety. In Thailand, this fresh tofu has only recently become available. Previously, the hard yellow type from China was used. In all the tofu recipes included here, fresh tofu can be used. The Japanese is probably the best.

♠ Son-in-Law Eggs

(*Kai Luk Koei*)
(color page 16)

This dish is an excellent accompaniment to a fiery curry. The bland eggs will help put out the flames.

SERVES 6–8

2 cups vegetable oil for deep-frying
8 hard-boiled eggs, peeled
1 medium onion, thinly sliced
3 dried or fresh red chili peppers
3–4 slices bacon

SAUCE
1 tsp All-Purpose Chili Sauce (see page 33)
3 Tbsps raw sugar
2 Tbsps fish soy (*nam pla*)
½ cup tamarind water (see page 12; substitute vinegar)

GARNISH
1 Tbsp chopped fresh coriander leaves

Put the oil in a deep-fryer or wok over medium-high heat and deep-fry the eggs in medium temperature (340° F/170° C) oil, turning carefully and frequently, until they are golden brown. Drain and set aside.

Fry the onion in the same oil until light brown; drain and set aside. Do the same with the chili peppers. Deep-fry the bacon and crumble it (there should be ½ cup).

In a separate pan or wok heat 2 Tbsps of the deep-frying oil and add all the SAUCE ingredients. Cook over low heat for 10 minutes, until thick.

Arrange the eggs on a plate or flat serving dish. Sprinkle with onion, chili peppers, and bacon before pouring the hot sauce over all. Garnish with coriander leaves and add a dash of pepper. Serve hot.

♠ Salted Eggs

(*Kai Kem*)

1 cup salt
3 cups boiling water
8 fresh chicken or duck eggs

Dissolve 1 cup salt in 3 cups boiling water. Cool. Add the eggs (be sure the water covers them) and keep them at room temperature for at least 2 weeks before using. They will keep safely for several weeks in the brine at room temperature and even longer if refrigerated. These are boiled and used in salads and are sometimes called for in Thai recipes.

♠ Egg Stew

Like the Pork, Chicken, and Egg Stew on page 137, this vegetarian dish can be prepared a day or a week ahead. Goes well with a green salad and rice or mashed potatoes.

SERVES 6–8

1 lb (450 gm) grilled tofu (*yaki dofu* in Japanese; substitute regular tofu)

1 lb (450 gm) daikon radish (substitute turnips or icicle radish)

10 hard-boiled eggs, peeled

2 tsps coarsely chopped coriander root

2 tsps coarsely chopped garlic

3 slices fresh ginger

½ tsp peppercorns, whole or freshly ground

3 Tbsps vegetable oil

SEASONINGS

3 Tbsps dark soy sauce

1 tsp Chinese five-spice powder

3 Tbsps fish soy (*nam pla*)

2 Tbsps raw sugar

Wrap the tofu in a clean kitchen towel, weight with 2 dinner plates, and drain for 1 hour. Peel the radish and cut it into 1½-inch (4-cm) cubes. Cut the tofu into pieces the same size. Put eggs, daikon, and tofu into a large saucepan.

Pound the coriander root, garlic, ginger, and peppercorns to a paste in a mortar. Fry the paste in the 3 Tbsps oil over medium heat until it releases its aroma—a few seconds only. Add this mixture to the eggs, daikon, and tofu. Blend gently but thoroughly.

Add the SEASONINGS along with 2 cups of water to the stew and simmer for 40 minutes over low heat.

This stew is best when left overnight and reheated the next day. Keeps 1 week refrigerated.

♠ Thai Omelette
(*Kai Yat Sai*)

Serve by itself for breakfast or as part of a curry meal. In Thailand this is usually accompanied by a chili sauce and Chilies in Vinegar (see page 9).

SERVES 6–8

FILLING

1 Tbsp vegetable oil

½ lb (225 gm) ground pork

½ medium onion, finely chopped
2 cloves garlic, finely chopped
½ medium tomato, coarsely chopped

SEASONINGS
2 tsps sugar
¼ tsp black pepper
2 tsps fish soy (*nam pla*)
1 tsp All-Purpose Chili Sauce (see page 33)

4 eggs
vegetable oil for frying omelettes

GARNISH
chopped fresh coriander leaves

Heat the Tbsp of oil in a frying pan over medium heat and stir-fry the pork just until it loses its color. Add chopped onion and garlic. Stir-fry for 2 minutes. Add the chopped tomatoes and all the SEASONINGS. Stir-fry about 3 minutes, until some of the tomato juice evaporates. Set aside.

Make an ordinary omelette with 2 of the eggs. Before folding it over, put half the FILLING inside the omelette. Repeat with the other 2 eggs and the remaining FILLING.

Garnish with fresh coriander leaves.

Variations
An equal amount of minced chicken or minced shrimp can be substituted for the ground pork.

⚜ Steamed Egg Custard with Red Curry
(*Haw Muk Kai*)

This is a very interesting and enjoyable dish, reminiscent of Japan's chawan-mushi *(savory steamed custard). It is an excellent accompaniment to a full Thai or western meal and is also fine for lunch.*

SERVES 6–8

1½ cups Chinese cabbage, cut into 1-inch (2-cm) squares
2 cups coconut milk
2–2½ Tbsps special red curry paste (see below)
2–2½ Tbsps fish soy (*nam pla*)
2 Tbsps rice flour
8 large fresh eggs

1 cup chopped collard greens (substitute chopped blanched spinach)
½ cup coconut cream
2 fresh (or dried) kaffir lime leaves (*bai makrut*), cut into fine slivers
2 green onions, chopped

8 custard cups

Blanch the Chinese cabbage by placing it in a bowl, pouring boiling water over it, and letting it sit for 1 minute. Drain and plunge into cold water. Squeeze out water.

Put the cabbage in a mixing bowl and add the 2 cups of coconut milk. Let sit for 3 minutes before mixing in the SPECIAL RED CURRY PASTE and fish soy. Blend in the rice flour, then break the 8 eggs into the mixture, taking great care not to break the yolks.

Blanch the collard greens in boiling water for 1 minute. Drain and squeeze dry. Divide the cooked collard greens among the 8 custard cups. Add 1 egg yolk to each cup and enough of the coconut milk mixture (with the Chinese cabbage) to fill the cups three-fourths full. Top them with 1 Tbsp of coconut cream. Sprinkle with a few shreds of kaffir lime leaf and green onion. Steam for 10–15 minutes, until the top of the custard appears dry. Serve hot or at room temperature.

SPECIAL RED CURRY PASTE

7 dried red chili peppers, seeded

8–10 shallots, coarsely chopped

6–8 cloves garlic, coarsely chopped

1 Tbsp finely chopped fresh lemon grass (or 1 tsp powdered)

4 slices fresh (or dried and soaked) galanga

5 coriander roots, coarsely chopped

½ tsp finely chopped kaffir lime peel (*makrut*)

2 slices fresh (or dried and soaked) *grachai* (*Kaempferia pandurata*)

5 peppercorns, whole or freshly ground

Blend all ingredients to a fine paste in a food processor or blender.

♠ Panang Curry with Peanuts and Eggs
(*Panang Kai*)

Here is an attractive and different egg dish. Goes with potatoes and green pasta as well as rice.

SERVES 6–8

3 cups coconut milk

2–3 Tbsps *Panang* Curry Paste (see page 29)

½ tsp sugar

2 Tbsps fish soy (*nam pla*)

8 hard-boiled eggs, peeled

1 cup fresh (or frozen) green peas

1 cup peanuts, coarsely chopped or crushed

GARNISHES

2 Tbsps chopped fresh coriander leaves

3 fresh red chili peppers, cut into fine slivers

In a frying pan, heat ½ cup of the coconut milk over medium-high heat and stir in the *Panang* Curry Paste. Cook it until the aroma is released (about 1 minute) and add the remaining 2½ cups coconut milk, the sugar, fish soy, eggs, and the peas. Cook for 6–8 minutes. Add the peanuts.

Remove the eggs from the rather soupy curry. Cut them in half lengthwise and place them cut side up in a shallow serving dish. Pour the curry gently around the eggs so that the yellow yolks contrast with the reddish curry. Sprinkle with coriander leaves and slivered chili peppers.

▲ Seafood Omelette

SERVES 6–8

2 cloves garlic, coarsely chopped

3–5 peppercorns, crushed

2 coriander roots, coarsely chopped

¼ cup vegetable oil

FILLING

1 cup cooked crab meat, cartilage removed

1 cup cooked shrimp, cut into rough chunks

½ cup fresh (or frozen) green peas, parboiled

2 green onions, coarsely chopped

2 Tbsps light soy sauce (or regular soy sauce)

pinch of salt

2 Tbsps vegetable oil

8 eggs, well beaten

GARNISH

2 Tbsps chopped fresh coriander leaves

Pound or blend the garlic, peppercorns, and coriander roots to a paste. Heat ¼ cup vegetable oil in a frying pan or wok over medium heat, add the paste, and stir-fry until the aroma is released—a few seconds. Add all the FILLING ingredients and stir-fry for 3–5 minutes. Set aside.

Put 2 Tbsps vegetable oil in a wok or frying pan over medium-high heat. Pour in half of the beaten eggs to cover the bottom of the pan or wok. Place half of the filling in the center, fold over the front and back then left and right. Turn the omelette (carefully) and fry the seamed side just until it *starts* to brown. (Depending on the heat, you might have to add a little more oil to fry the other side.) Repeat with the remaining ingredients to make a second omelette. Place both omelettes on a serving plate and sprinkle with fresh coriander and add a dash of white pepper. An excellent dish for Sunday brunch.

♠ Crispy Eggs with Crab

When you are confronted with two hot curries, something bland yet interesting is called for. This dish qualifies. Also good for breakfast or as a filling in hot toasted sandwiches.

SERVES 6–8

6 or 7 eggs
1½ cups cooked crab meat, cartilage removed
½ cup chopped green onion
1½ Tbsps fish soy (*nam pla*)
½ tsp pepper

½ cup vegetable oil
2 Tbsps crushed garlic

GARNISH
2 Tbsps chopped fresh coriander leaves

Beat the eggs until frothy. Add the crab, green onion, fish soy, and pepper and beat again.

In a wok or frying pan, heat the ½ cup of vegetable oil over medium-high heat. Add the crushed garlic and stir-fry until it starts to brown—about 30 seconds. Pour the egg mixture into the pan. Do not stir at all. When bubbles appear, turn the egg over and continue cooking until it appears almost dry. The entire cooking time should not exceed 3 minutes.

Sprinkle with fresh coriander leaves. Serve hot.

Variation
Instead of crab, use an equal amount of raw chicken breast cut into strips.

♠ Flowers and Eggs (an Omelette)

SERVES 6–8

7 eggs
½ cup fresh shrimp (substitute shiitake mushrooms)

½ cup vegetable oil
½ medium onion, chopped
½–1 tsp cayenne pepper
1 cup small cauliflower florets
½ cup small broccoli florets
¼ tsp pepper
½ tsp salt

GARNISH
2 green onions, chopped

Beat the eggs until frothy. Shell, devein, and chop the shrimp.

Heat ¼ cup of the oil in a frying pan or wok over high heat. Add the onions and cayenne pepper, vegetables, and shrimp. Stir-fry 3–5 minutes. Add the egg all at once and sprinkle with the salt and pepper. Stir through the eggs 2–3 times with a wooden spoon. Drizzle the remaining ¼ cup oil around the edge of the pan and let the egg cook undisturbed 1–2 minutes. Turn the heat off and let it sit for 1 more minute.

Place in a serving dish and sprinkle with green onions. Serve hot.

▲ The Chicken and The Egg

If you have any leftover roast chicken (or even leftover roast pork), use it here instead of the chicken breast. Good for breakfast, lunch, and sandwiches.

SERVES 6–8

⅓ cup vegetable oil
2 cloves garlic, crushed
1½ cups coarsely chopped chicken breast meat
6 or 7 eggs, well beaten
pinch of salt
½ tsp pepper
1 tsp fish soy (*nam pla*)

GARNISH
2 green onions, chopped

Pour the vegetable oil into a frying pan or wok and stir-fry the garlic and chicken for 1–2 minutes over high heat. Pour in the beaten egg and sprinkle the salt, pepper, and fish soy over the top. Stir-fry for 2–3 minutes, until the egg appears slightly dry. Place on a serving dish and sprinkle with the green onion. Add a final sprinkle of black pepper and serve.

▲ Tofu with Saifun Noodles

SERVES 6–8

1½ lbs (700 gm) regular tofu (Japanese "cotton" tofu)
1 cup fresh (or dried) shiitake mushrooms
3 oz (90 gm) saifun noodles (Japanese *harusame*)
4 Tbsps vegetable oil
2 cloves garlic, crushed
½ cup dried shrimp, rinsed
1 cup fresh (or frozen) green peas, parboiled
½ tsp pepper
½ tsp salt
1 Tbsp fish soy (*nam pla*)
2 Tbsps sesame oil

Cut the tofu into 1-inch (2-cm) cubes. (Reconstitute dried mushrooms for 30 minutes in tepid water.) Remove stems of mushrooms and cut caps into quarters. Soak the saifun noodles in boiling water for 10 minutes.

Put the 4 Tbsps oil in a frying pan or wok over high heat. Add the crushed garlic and stir-fry just until it begins to change color. Add tofu, mushrooms, and dried shrimp and stir-fry for 3–5 minutes. Add the saifun noodles and peas along with 2 Tbsps water, the pepper and salt, fish soy, and sesame oil and stir-fry 5 more minutes.

Serve very hot. Add a dash of black pepper just before serving.

▲ Tofu with Sour Curry

If you live in an area where Mexican condiments are readily available, substitute an equal amount of Salsa Ranchera La Victoria sauce for the sour curry paste. The results are equally good.

SERVES 6–8

2 lbs (1 kg) regular tofu (Japanese "cotton" tofu)

½ cup vegetable oil

½ cup chopped onion

1–2 Tbsps Sour Curry Paste (see page 27)

¼ lb (115 gm) okra, cut into ½-inch (1-cm) pieces

3 medium tomatoes, each cut into 8 wedges

2 Tbsps cornstarch dissolved in ½ cup water

1 Tbsp lime (or lemon) juice

⅓ tsp salt

1½ Tbsps fish soy (*nam pla*)

GARNISH

2 green onions, chopped

Cut the tofu into ½ × 1 × 1½-inch (1 × 2 × 4-cm) pieces. Drain in a colander for 10 minutes. Put the ½ cup vegetable oil in a frying pan or wok over medium heat. Add the chopped onion and stir-fry for 1–2 minutes. Add the tofu, spreading it out evenly in the bottom of the wok, and fry it just until it begins to change color. Turn it over and fry the other side. Remove the tofu.

Add the curry paste and stir-fry for 1 minute. Put the tofu back in the wok and add the okra and tomatoes. Stir-fry, taking care not to break the tofu, for 3–4 minutes.

Dissolve the cornstarch in the water and add it along with the lime (or lemon) juice, salt, and fish soy. Let the mixture cook for 5–7 minutes over medium heat, stirring frequently. Just before serving, add the chopped green onion. Serve hot with rice.

♠ Sweet-and-Sour Tofu

SERVES 6–8

4 oz (120 gm) fresh (or dried) shiitake mushrooms
2 lbs (1 kg) regular tofu (Japanese "cotton" tofu)
2 Japanese cucumbers (or small western cucumbers), peeled
1 green pepper
3 medium tomatoes, each cut into 8 wedges
½ cup vegetable oil
2 cloves garlic, crushed

SEASONINGS
2 Tbsps soy sauce
1 Tbsp sugar
1 Tbsp tomato paste
1½ Tbsps cornstarch dissolved in ¾ cup water
½ tsp pepper
2 tsps All-Purpose Chili Sauce (see page 33)
dash lemon juice

GARNISH
2 green onions, chopped into 1-inch (2-cm) lengths

Remove the shiitake mushroom stems and cut the caps into 1-inch (2-cm) chunks. (If using dried shiitake, soak them in warm water for 30 minutes first.)

Wrap the tofu in a clean kitchen towel and weight with 2 dinner plates for 30 minutes to drain and make the tofu firmer. Cut the tofu into ½ × 1 × 1½-inch (1 × 2 × 4-cm) pieces.

Quarter the cucumbers lengthwise and cut these quarters into 1½-inch (4-cm) lengths. Cut the green pepper into 1 × 2-inch (2 × 5-cm) chunks.

Heat the ½ cup oil in a wok or large frying pan over medium-high heat. Add the tofu and carefully stir-fry until the color changes. Take care not to break the pieces. Remove the tofu and add the garlic. Stir-fry until the color changes.

Add all the vegetables to the pan with the garlic in it and stir-fry for 2 minutes. Put the tofu back into the pan with the vegetables, and add all the SEASONINGS. Stir-fry for 3–5 minutes, until the liquid thickens.

Place in a serving dish and sprinkle with green onion.

♠ Tofu with Shrimp

This is a mild, nourishing dish for fussy eaters. And, it is easy to prepare. A mild dish traditionally accompanies a classic Thai curry dinner.

2 lbs (1 kg) regular tofu (Japanese "cotton" tofu)

¼ lb (115 gm) white-fleshed fish fillet

½ lb (225 gm) fresh shrimp

1 Tbsp ginger juice (see page 10)

1 Tbsp saké

1½ Tbsps cornstarch

½ cup vegetable oil

1 Tbsp finely chopped garlic

1 generous Tbsp Chinese pickle (Tientsin Preserved Vegetable)

¼ tsp pepper

½ tsp salt

3 iceberg lettuce leaves, torn into bite-sized pieces

GARNISH

2 green onions, chopped

Wrap the tofu in a clean kitchen towel, weight with a dinner plate or two, and let sit for 10 minutes. Cut the tofu into 1 × 1 × 1½-inch (2 × 2 × 4-cm) pieces. Cut the fish into ¼ × ¼ × 1½-inch (¾ × ¾ × 4-cm) strips.

Shell the shrimp, slit the backs open, and devein. Marinate the fish and shrimp in the ginger juice for 2–3 minutes. Add the saké and marinate 2–3 more minutes. Sprinkle with the cornstarch and mix well (hands are best for this).

Put the ½ cup of oil in a frying pan or wok over medium heat, add the garlic, and stir-fry just until it begins to change color. Add the tofu and stir-fry gently for 3–5 minutes, until it starts to turn golden. Remove the tofu, add the fish and shrimp and 2 Tbsps water and stir-fry for 3 minutes. Add the Chinese pickle, salt, and pepper, and ½ cup water. Stir-fry for 2 minutes. Return the tofu, heat, and add the lettuce. Stir quickly for 2 or 3 turns only.

Transfer to a serving dish. Sprinkle with chopped green onion and serve hot.

▲ Steamed Tofu with Shrimp and Pork
(Tow Hoo Nung)

2 lbs (1 kg) regular tofu (Japanese "cotton" tofu)

½ lb (225 gm) medium shrimp

¼ lb (115 gm) ground pork

1 egg, lightly beaten

2 Tbsps soy sauce

½ tsp pepper

1–2 cloves garlic, finely chopped

1 Tbsp Chinese pickle (Tientsin Preserved Vegetable; optional)
2 tsps finely chopped ginger
½ cup julienned celery

GARNISH
2 green onions, cut into 1½-inch (4-cm) lengths

Mash the tofu well with a fork. Shell and devein the shrimp and chop very coarsely. Add the shrimp, pork, beaten egg, soy sauce, pepper, and garlic to the tofu. Mix well.

Place the mixture in a heatproof container (a soufflé dish is good) and sprinkle with the Chinese pickle, ginger, and celery. Place the container in a hot steamer and steam over medium heat for 12–15 minutes.

A toothpick inserted in the middle will come out clean when it is done. Do not overcook, because the tofu gets tough. Turn the heat off, remove container from steamer, sprinkle with green onion, and serve hot.

▲ Tofu and Mushrooms in Mustard Sauce

This is a non-Thai dish, but a creative way to entertain vegetarians.

SERVES 6–8

2 Tbsps vegetable oil
2 lbs (1 kg) regular tofu (Japanese ''cotton'' tofu), cut into
    ½ × 1 × 1½-inch (1 × 2 × 4-cm) pieces
½ lb (225 gm) button mushrooms

2 Tbsps vegetable oil
½ cup flour
2 chicken bouillon cubes dissolved in ½ cup water
3 Tbsps soy sauce
½ tsp pepper
2 Tbsps Gray Poupon mustard

GARNISHES
3 green onions, cut into 1½-inch (4-cm) pieces
1 Tbsp chopped fresh coriander leaves

In a frying pan heat 2 Tbsps oil to medium hot, add the tofu pieces and fry carefully just until they change color. Remove the tofu and lightly sauté the mushrooms. Remove the mushrooms and make a modified white sauce by heating the second 2 Tbsps vegetable oil over medium-high heat, blending in the flour, then blending in the bouillon, soy sauce, pepper, and mustard.

Put the tofu and mushrooms back into the white sauce, cover the pan, and cook over very low heat for 15 minutes.

Place in a serving dish and sprinkle with the onion and coriander. Serve hot.

▲ Stuffed Tofu

Here is another dish adapted from Chinese cuisine. The flavor and texture contrasts create interest, and strong spices are avoided.

SERVES 6–8

2 lbs (1 kg) regular tofu (Japanese "cotton" tofu)

FILLING

5 oz (150 gm) ground pork

2 cloves garlic, finely chopped

1 Tbsp fish soy (*nam pla*)

½ tsp pepper

1 tsp finely chopped coriander root

2 eggs, well beaten

2 cups vegetable oil for deep-frying

GARNISH

1 Tbsp chopped fresh coriander leaves

Cut the tofu into 1½-inch (4-cm) cubes. Slit each block almost through the middle.

Mix the FILLING ingredients well and stuff 2 tsps into the slit in each piece of tofu.

Coat the stuffed tofu cubes with the beaten egg. Deep-fry in hot oil (360° F/185° C) for 2–3 minutes. Fry only 4 or 5 pieces at a time or they will stick together. Drain.

Sprinkle with the coriander leaves and serve hot or at room temperature with the DIPPING SAUCE as an hors d'oeuvre or part of a Thai meal.

DIPPING SAUCE

3 dried red chili peppers, seeded, soaked, and coarsely chopped

2 cloves garlic, coarsely chopped

1½ Tbsps sugar

4 Tbsps vinegar

2 Tbsps fish soy (*nam pla*)

Pound or blend the chili peppers and garlic and sugar to a smooth paste. Blend in the vinegar and fish soy.

Variation
Instead of pork, use an equal amount of fish or shrimp.

SEAFOOD

อาหารทะเล

In a country with a long coastline and a love of good food, it is only natural that all kinds of fish and seafood play an important part in the Thai diet. The plenty and ubiquity is evidenced in a Thai song, which starts, "*Nai naam mi pla, nai na mi khaw*"—"In the water there are fish, in the fields there is rice"—celebrating the people's recognition of the abundance their land offers.

Inland, freshwater fish are important, as are ocean fish preserved in all the ways they can be preserved.

Fresh fish are prepared in essentially two ways in Thai cooking—in curries and grilled over charcoal. In the latter method, the fish is not seasoned before or during grilling. Rather, the grilled fish is dipped into a sauce of some kind. The simplest sauce for this purpose is a hot-salty-sweet-sour combination (chopped chili peppers; fish soy; tamarind water or lemon juice; sugar); more complex sauces are found on pages 33-39.

Seafood also forms the basis for two of Southeast Asia's ubiquitous condiments—fish soy (Thai: *nam pla*) and shrimp paste (Thai: *kapi*; recipe on page 11). Fish soy is made from heavily salted fish, which are allowed to age; the resulting liquid is filtered off. The flavor is rich and salty, resembling soy sauce (hence its name here), and not remotely fishy. This is essentially the same sauce as the ancient Roman *garum* or *liquamen* and has a history of great antiquity in Southeast Asia. Similar sauces are made from shrimp and squid.

♠ Mussels with Sour Curry
(color page 17)

This unusual mussel dish with a thick sauce is delightful as an hors d'oeuvre as well as a fish course.

SERVES 8

7 lbs (3 kg) steamed mussels

4 cups coconut milk

3 Tbsps flour

2 eggs, lightly beaten

3 Tbsps Sour Curry Paste (see page 27)

1 Tbsp fish soy (*nam pla*)

2 Tbsps white wine

½ tsp sugar

GARNISH

5 fresh or dried red chili peppers, cut into needle-thin slivers

Clean the mussels and steam them (use your favorite method) for 5 minutes over high heat. Discard any that do not open during steaming. Remove the mussels from their shells, split the double shells in two at the hinge, and save 24 of the largest shells for serving. Place the meat of 2 or 3 mussels in each half shell, arrange them neatly in a baking dish or jellyroll pan and set aside.

Prepare the sauce by warming the coconut milk, flour, and beaten eggs over medium heat. Add the curry paste, fish soy, wine, and sugar and bring the mixture to a boil over medium heat. Reduce the heat to low and cook the sauce for 3–5 minutes. Divide half of the sauce between the shells containing the mussels, being sure to cover each shell (containing the meat of 2 or 3 mussels) with some of the sauce. Bake in a 400° F (205°C) oven for 10 minutes or until surface of sauce begins to brown.

Keep the remaining sauce warm while the mussels bake. Warm 8 plates. Put 4 Tbsps of sauce in each plate, add 3 of the baked mussel shells and sprinkle with needle-fine slivers of red chili. Serve hot.

♠ Steamed Herbed Mussels
(*Hoy Mang Pu Naung*)

SERVES 6–8

5 lbs (2 kg) medium-sized fresh mussels

1 cup fresh sweet basil leaves

4 green onions, cut into 1½-inch (4-cm) lengths

DIPPING SAUCE

½ cup lemon juice

2 Tbsps fish soy (*nam pla*)

1 tsp sugar

2 coriander roots, coarsely chopped

111

3 cloves garlic, crushed
1 tsp red pepper flakes

Wash the mussels well. Heat a steamer and add the mussels. Sprinkle the basil and green onion over the mussels, then steam about 10 minutes or until the mussels open. Discard any that do not open.

Turn the heat off and let the mussels sit 2 minutes before opening the steamer lid.

While the mussels are cooking, whir all the DIPPING SAUCE ingredients with 3 Tbsps hot water in a blender or food processor (or pound in a mortar) to form a rough paste.

Serve the mussels hot with the sauce in a small bowl. Use toothpicks, a fork, or chopsticks to dip the mussels.

♠ Fried Fish Cakes
(*Thod Man Pla*)

SERVES 8–10

SEASONINGS
2 Tbsps salt water (dissolve ¼ tsp salt in 2 Tbsps water)
1 tsp sugar
1½ Tbsps fish soy (*nam pla*)
1½–2 Tbsps Red Curry Paste (see page 24)

2 lbs (1 kg) white-fleshed fish fillets, ground or processed to a paste

½ lb (225 gm) green beans, finely chopped
2–3 cups vegetable oil for deep-frying

3 cups Cucumber Pickle (either of the two on page 73)

Mix the SEASONINGS and add them to the fish. With a wooden spoon, beat until sticky—about 50 strokes.

Add the chopped green beans and mix thoroughly. Form into small round or oval cakes 2 inches (5 cm) across and ¼ inch (¾ cm) thick.

Heat the oil to hot (360° F/180° C) and deep-fry the fish cakes, turning only once, until both sides are light gold. Drain well.

Serve with either Cucumber Pickle. Most Thais prefer to dip the fish cakes right into the vinegar that is part of the pickle, so it is best to serve several small bowls of the pickle.

♠ Fried Shrimp Cakes
(*Thod Man Gung*)

The best version of these variations on the more traditional fried fish cakes has to be that served at the Petchtapee Restaurant in Surat Thani, a southern

Thai town undistinguished except for the fact that it serves as a landing for tourist ferries. This recipe was obtained from the chef there.

MAKES 12–14 CAKES

1 lb (450 gm) medium shrimp, shelled and deveined

½ lb (225 gm) pork fat (or a very fatty cut), cut into bite-sized pieces

2 Tbsps cornstarch

¼ tsp Thai black pepper (substitute any black pepper)

2 Tbsps fish soy (*nam pla*)

1 Tbsp sugar

1 cup dry bread crumbs

4–5 Tbsps vegetable oil

Place the shrimp and pork in a food processor and add the cornstarch, salt, pepper, fish soy, and sugar. Using the pulse function, carefully process until a rough paste is formed. Be careful not to over-process. Chunks of shrimp and fat should remain. (Work with a very sharp Chinese cleaver can replace the food processor.)

Form into 3-inch (8-cm) patties and coat them with bread crumbs. Heat the oil in a frying pan over high heat and fry the cakes until golden on each side (about 3 minutes). (Or, deep-fry them in hot [360° F/180° C] oil.)

Serve hot as part of a Thai or western meal. Choose any kind of dipping sauce. A good one is bottled Thai sweet chili sauce for fish, which is available in many oriental markets.

⛰ Choo Chee Curry with Fish
(*Gang Choo Chee*)

This curry has a thick sauce and goes well with plain rice or fine noodles (any kind).

SERVES 6–8

8 small trout (fresh or frozen) or 1 2-lb (1-kg) whole red snapper

3 Tbsps vegetable oil

1 cup coconut cream

2–3 Tbsps *Choo Chee* Curry Paste (see page 26)

2 cups coconut milk

2 Tbsps fish soy (*nam pla*)

2 tsps raw sugar

GARNISH

1 fresh kaffir lime leaf (*bai makrut*), cut into fine slivers (optional)

Clean the fish inside and out, leaving heads and tails intact. Score the fish diagonally 2–3 times on each side.

Heat the oil over medium-high heat in a wok or frying pan. Fry each fish on each side until the skin is crisp. Set aside.

In a large pan, heat the cup of coconut cream over medium heat and add the curry paste. Cook until the curry paste releases its aroma, about 1 minute. Add the fish, coconut milk, fish soy, and sugar. Cook over low heat for 10 minutes.

Place in a serving dish and sprinkle with kaffir lime leaf slivers. Serve hot with rice.

Variation
Use 1 lb (450 gm) of mushrooms (any kind) and ½ lb (225 gm) fresh shrimp (shelled and deveined) instead of fish. Add mushrooms to coconut cream/curry paste mixture and cook 3 minutes. Then add shrimp with coconut milk, fish soy, and sugar and cook 5 minutes (not 10 minutes).

▲ Red Curry with Shrimp and Pineapple
(*Gang Pet Gung*)
(color page 13)

The other red curries in this book are hot, but this one is not. It is rich, sweet, piquant, and juicy.

SERVES 6

1½ lbs (700 gm) medium shrimp
¼ cup coconut cream
3–3½ Tbsps Red Curry Paste (see page 24)
3 cups fresh pineapple, cut into ½-inch (1-cm) chunks
2 cups coconut milk
½ cup dried shrimp, rinsed and lightly pounded
2–2½ Tbsps fish soy (*nam pla*)
1 Tbsp sugar
1 cup additional coconut cream
2 fresh kaffir lime leaves (*bai makrut*), torn into small shreds (optional)

Shell and devein shrimp, leaving the tails intact.

Place the ¼ cup coconut cream in a saucepan and stir in the curry paste. Add the pineapple and cook over medium heat for 3 minutes. Add the 2 cups of coconut milk and dried shrimp and cook 5 minutes over low heat, stirring occasionally. Add the fresh shrimp, fish soy, and sugar. Bring just to a boil, then add the final cup of coconut cream and the shredded kaffir lime leaves.

Serve with hot rice or very fine noodles (Italian vermicelli or Japanese *somen*).

Note: The shredded kaffir lime leaves are not essential for the flavor of the curry but are a nice addition.

♠ Stir-Fried Shrimp with Lemon Grass

(color page 18)

SERVES 8

A MIXTURE

1 Tbsp finely chopped fresh lemon grass (or 1 tsp powdered)
1 Tbsp finely chopped garlic
1½ tsps peppercorns, whole or freshly ground
½ tsp salt
4 dried red chili peppers, seeded, soaked, and coarsely chopped

B MIXTURE

3–4 Tbsps fish soy (*nam pla*) (depending on desired saltiness)
1 Tbsp sugar
1 Tbsp cornstarch dissolved in 2 Tbsps water

4 Tbsps vegetable oil

2 lbs (1 kg) large shrimp, shelled and deveined
¼ lb (115 gm) button mushrooms, cut in half
¼ lb (115 gm) snow peas, stringed

GARNISHES

¼ cup coarsely chopped or crushed peanuts
2 Tbsps slivered green onion tops

Pound the A MIXTURE ingredients to a paste in a mortar or whir in a blender or food processor.

Mix the B MIXTURE and set aside.

Heat the oil in a frying pan or wok over medium-high heat. Add the A MIXTURE and stir-fry until the aroma is released—only a few seconds. Increase the heat to high and stir-fry the shrimp, mushrooms, and snow peas for 3 minutes. Add the B MIXTURE and blend well.

Transfer to a serving dish and sprinkle with the crushed peanuts and slivered onion tops before serving. Can be eaten with rice or fried fine noodles.

♠ Gang Liang Curry with Fish and Spinach

(*Gang Liang Pla*)

This is a very soupy curry. In fact you can reduce the Gang Liang *Curry Paste to 1 Tbsp and serve this as a soup.*

SERVES 6–8

1 lb (450 gm) spinach, fresh or frozen
¼ lb (115 gm) smoked fish (any smoked fish is good; the traditional
    Thai fish for this dish is *pra chalad*, "featherback" fish)
¼ lb (115 gm) cooked shrimp
2–3 Tbsps *Gang Liang* Curry Paste (see page 29)

5 cups coconut milk

2½ Tbsps fish soy (*nam pla*)

GARNISH

¼ cup fresh sweet basil leaves

Clean the spinach and trim off the stems. Blanch in an ample amount of boiling water. (It is not necessary to blanch frozen spinach.) Plunge into cold water, drain, and gently squeeze out water.

Tear or cut the smoked fish into small bite-sized pieces. Whir fish, shrimp, and curry paste together in a blender or pound in a mortar.

Bring the 5 cups of coconut milk to a simmer over medium heat. Add the spinach, the smoked fish-shrimp-curry mixture, and the fish soy. Reduce the heat to low and simmer for 5 to 7 minutes.

Remove to a serving dish and sprinkle with shredded fresh basil. Serve hot with rice.

▲ Sour Curry with Fish Balls
(*Gang Som Luk Chin Pla*)

A vegetable called phak boong, *which grows in water like watercress, is traditionally used in this dish.* Phak boong *is hard to find outside Southeast Asia, so tender spinach that has been blanched makes a good substitute.*

SERVES 6–8

1 lb (450 gm) white-fleshed fish fillet(s) (any fish will do), skin removed

½ tsp finely chopped coriander root

5 peppercorns, whole or freshly ground

pinch of salt

2-oz (60-gm) piece of fresh tuna

2–3 Tbsps Sour Curry Paste (see page 27)

½ lb (225 gm) spinach, blanched and cut into 1½-inch (4-cm) lengths

5 cups coconut milk

4–5 Tbsps tamarind water (see page 12)

2½ Tbsps fish soy (*nam pla*)

1 Tbsp sugar

In a blender or food processor, whir the white fish with the coriander root, peppercorns, and salt to make a paste. Shape the paste into fish balls about ½ inch (1 cm) in diameter. Set aside.

Lightly grill the piece of fresh tuna and pound or blend it with the Sour Curry Paste.

Heat the 5 cups of coconut milk in a medium-sized saucepan over medium heat. Dissolve the tuna and curry paste mixture in the coconut milk and add the fish balls and spinach. Add the tamarind water, the fish soy, and sugar to the curry blend and cook until the fish balls are done—about 3 minutes. Adjust the seasoning to taste.

Serve hot with rice.

☙ Yellow Curry with Swordfish
(*Gang Luang Pla*)

This has a pleasant, slightly sour taste and is eaten with plain boiled rice.

SERVES 6–8

1½ lbs (700 gm) swordfish steaks
¼ lb (115 gm) zucchini
¼ lb (115 gm) tomatoes, peeled
2 oz (60 gm) green beans

2½–3 Tbsps Yellow Curry Paste (see page 25)

SEASONINGS
2½ Tbsps fish soy (*nam pla*)
2 tsps sugar
2 Tbsps tamarind water (see page 12)

Wash the fish steaks and cut them into 1-inch (2-cm) pieces. Cut the zucchini lengthwise into ½-inch (1-cm) thick slices. Cut the tomatoes into 1-inch (2-cm) chunks and snap the green beans into 1-inch (2-cm) lengths.

Bring 6 cups of water to boil over high heat. Add one-third of the fish and boil it for 3 minutes. Reduce the heat to low and remove the fish. Combine it with the curry paste to make a thick but smooth paste.

Put the paste back in the water along with vegetables, remaining two-thirds of the fish, and the SEASONINGS. Cook over low heat for 5 to 7 minutes. Serve hot.

☙ Fried Fish with Fresh Young Ginger
(*Pla Pat King*)

SERVES 6–8

2 lbs (1 kg) whole white-fleshed fish (3–4 fish)
1 cup vegetable oil for deep-frying
2 Tbsps needle-slivered ginger (young ginger preferred)
3–4 cloves garlic
3 slices lean bacon, cut into julienne strips

SEASONINGS
2 Tbsps fish soy (*nam pla*)
½ tsp black pepper
½ tsp sugar

GARNISH
2 green onions, cut into 1½-inch (4-cm) lengths

Scale, clean, and wash the fish but leave them whole (with heads and tails intact). In a deep-fryer or wok, heat oil to hot (360° F/180° C). Score the fish 2–3 times on each side, pat dry, and fry both sides until lightly browned. Set aside and keep warm in a serving dish.

In a separate frying pan, heat 3 Tbsps of the oil you fried the fish in over medium-high heat and add the ginger and garlic. Stir-fry for 1 minute. Add the julienned bacon and stir-fry for 2 minutes. Add ½ cup of water and all the SEASONINGS. Bring to a boil and pour over the fried fish.

Serve as hot as possible. Garnish with green onion and add a sprinkle of freshly ground black pepper over the fish before bringing it to the table.

♠ Eel with Ginger

Although this is a Thai recipe, Japanese (unagi), French, or American eel is preferable to the Thai eels.

SERVES 6–8

3 cloves garlic, coarsely chopped
2 coriander roots, coarsely chopped
5–6 peppercorns, whole or freshly ground

¼ cup vegetable oil

1 lb (450 gm) fresh eel, cut into 1½-inch (4-cm) squares

SEASONINGS
1 Tbsp rice vinegar
½ tsp salt
1½ Tbsps finely julienned fresh ginger

1 Tbsp sesame oil
2 green onions, cut into 1½-inch (4-cm) lengths

GARNISH
3–4 red chili peppers, cut into fine slivers

In a blender, food processor, or mortar, make a paste of the garlic, coriander root, and peppercorns.

Add the ¼ cup oil to a frying pan or wok over medium heat and stir-fry the paste until the aroma is released—a few seconds only. Turn the heat up to high, add the eel, and stir-fry for 2 or 3 minutes.

Add SEASONINGS all at once and stir-fry for 5 minutes. Add the sesame oil, remove from heat, add green onion, and stir through twice only.

Remove to a serving dish and sprinkle with red chili pepper slivers for decoration—it is not necessary to eat them. Serve with hot rice.

♠ Sardines with Mint
(color page 15)

This is a cross between a salad and a fish dish. Easy to prepare, exotic, and delicious, it is good on buffets, for lunch, and summer dinners.

2 15-oz cans sardines in tomato sauce
½ cup parched rice, crushed (see below)
6 shallots, thinly sliced (substitute ½ cup thinly sliced red onion)
1 Tbsp finely chopped fresh lemon grass
1 Tbsp finely chopped ginger

SEASONINGS
1–1½ Tbsps fish soy (*nam pla*)
juice of ½ lime (or lemon)
½ tsp sugar
½–1 Tbsp red pepper flakes

GARNISHES
1½ Tbsps chopped fresh coriander leaves
5–6 fresh or dried guinea peppers (*prik kee nu*), finely chopped
½ cup fresh mint leaves, roughly torn

Place the sardines in a bowl.

Add ½ cup of dry rice (either long grain or short grain) to a frying pan (without oil) and parch it over medium heat, shaking the pan until the rice starts to turn golden. Remove from heat and coarsely crush in a mortar.

Add the shallots, lemon grass, and ginger to the sardines. Add the SEASONINGS and mix gently. (Of course the sardines will lose their shape.)

Place in a serving dish and sprinkle with coriander leaves, guinea pepper, parched rice, and mint. Serve as part of a meal or as an unusual hors d'oeuvre with crackers or thinly sliced party rye.

♨ Simple Spiced Eel

The richness of eel lends itself to Thai flavors. This is an original, Thai style dish.

4 Tbsps vegetable oil
1½ lbs (700 gm) eel (cooked or raw), cut into 1-inch (2-cm) squares
2 Tbsps *Panang* Curry Paste (see page 29)
3–4 mixed fresh red and green chili peppers, coarsely chopped
½ tsp sugar
1½–2 Tbsps fish soy (*nam pla*)
2 fresh (or dried) kaffir lime leaves (*bai makrut*), cut into fine slivers

Pour the oil into a frying pan or wok over high heat. When the oil is hot, add all ingredients plus 2 Tbsps water and stir-fry for 2 or 3 minutes only. Serve hot with rice.

♠ Steamed Fish Custard
(Ho Mok Pla)

Eat this with spoons. With a green salad, a green vegetable, and good crusty bread, this dish makes a memorable meal.

1⅓ lbs (600 gm) fish fillets, such as sole, red snapper, sea bass,
    fresh tuna (shrimp also works well)
2½–3 Tbsps Red Curry Paste (see page 24)
2½ cups coconut cream
3 Tbsps fish soy (*nam pla*)
1 Tbsp sugar
2 eggs, well beaten

3 Tbsps flour

½ cup sweet basil leaves
2 cups coarsely shredded Chinese cabbage

GARNISHES
2 Tbsps chopped fresh coriander leaves
3 fresh kaffir lime leaves (*bai makrut*), cut into fine slivers (optional)
4–5 fresh red chili peppers, cut into fine slivers

Clean the fish fillets (or shrimp) and cut the fish into ½ × 1 × 1½-inch (1 × 2 × 4-cm) pieces. Place the fish pieces in a large mixing bowl and add the curry paste. Using a wooden spoon, gently mix the curry paste and fish for at least 2 minutes. Add 2 cups of the coconut cream and stir gently 3 more minutes. The mixture will thicken while you stir. Take care not to mash the fish pieces. Add the fish soy and sugar and stir. Now add the 2 beaten eggs and stir until the eggs are completely blended into the mixture.

Make the topping by blending 3 Tbsps flour with the remaining ½ cup of coconut cream. Set aside.

Coarsely chop the sweet basil. Blanch the Chinese cabbage in boiling water for 1 minute. Squeeze and set aside while you heat the steamer.

Divide the Chinese cabbage among 10 cupcake-size foil cups. Divide the sweet basil evenly among the cups also, then fill the cups about three-fourths full with the fish mixture. Top this off with 1 Tbsp of the topping mixture and sprinkle with chopped coriander, kaffir lime leaf slivers, and chili pepper slivers. Steam the fish custards for 15 minutes (do not overcook, or they will lose their flavor). Serve warm or at room temperature.

♠ Nam Ya Curry with Lobster

Serve this luxurious dish with crusty French bread or warm rolls as the fish course of a western meal or light lunch all by itself. An example of Thai-French or French-Thai cooking.

3 fresh or frozen large whole lobsters
2 Tbsps good-quality white wine
pinch of salt

4 Tbsps vegetable oil
2½ cups coconut milk
3 oz (90 gm) small shrimp, shelled and deveined
1 Tbsp *Nam Ya* Curry Paste (see page 28)
2 Tbsps fish soy (*nam pla*)
3 Tbsps tomato sauce (optional)
2 tsps sugar (optional)

GARNISH
10–12 fresh sweet basil leaves

Cut each lobster in half lengthwise (with shell), and marinate in the wine and salt for 10 minutes.

Heat the 4 Tbsps vegetable oil over medium heat in a large pot or wok, add lobster halves, cover, and cook (in effect, this is steaming) until the lobster is just cooked through. Set aside.

Put the coconut milk in a medium-sized saucepan and bring to a boil over medium heat. Add the shrimp, and when the coconut milk just comes to a second boil, turn off the heat. Remove the shrimp to a blender or food processor and make a fine paste. Return this paste to the coconut milk along with the curry paste, fish soy, tomato sauce (optional) and sugar (optional). Bring just to a boil over medium heat. Taste for seasoning—the sauce should be very mild.

Place each warm lobster half on a heated plate, pour on sauce in an attractive way, and garnish with basil leaves. Serve hot.

▲ Steamed Prawns in Sour Curry

Here is an uncomplicated, luxurious, and different dish for seafood lovers. Goes beautifully with either pommes Anna *or plain boiled rice.*

SERVES 6

12–14 very large prawns (at least 4 in/10 cm long)
24 fresh button mushrooms
2 Tbsps white wine
pinch of salt

SAUCE
2½ cups coconut milk
3 oz (90 gm) white-fleshed fish fillet
1 Tbsp chopped onion
2 Tbsps Sour Curry Paste (see page 27)

1 medium tomato, peeled and seeded

¼ tsp salt

½ tsp sugar

<small>GARNISH</small>

6 sprigs watercress

Shell the prawns but leave the tails intact, then slit down the back and devein. Pat dry, then sprinkle with wine and the pinch of salt.

Preheat a steamer. Place the shrimp and mushrooms in the hot steamer. Steam for 3 minutes over high heat. Turn the heat off and let the shrimp and mushrooms sit for 5 minutes.

Meanwhile prepare the SAUCE. Place the coconut milk in a medium saucepan. Cook the fish in lightly salted boiling water for 3 minutes. Drain. Put the fish in a blender or food processor and add the onion, curry paste, and tomato. Blend to a smooth paste and add it to the coconut milk. Bring the sauce to a boil over medium heat and boil gently for 2 minutes. Add the ¼ tsp salt and ½ tsp sugar. Adjust the seasonings.

Warm 6 serving plates. Put the prawns and mushrooms in the middle (2 prawns for the heartier appetites) and divide the sauce evenly among the 6 servings. Garnish each plate with a sprig of watercress.

♠ Sour Curry with Fish and Daikon Radish
(Gang Som Pla)

SERVES 6–8

1½ lbs (700 gm) mild white-fleshed fish fillets (or fresh tuna)

10 oz (300 gm) daikon radish (substitute turnips or icicle radish)

½ lb (225 gm) tomatoes

2½–3 Tbsps Sour Curry Paste (see page 27)

<small>SEASONINGS</small>

2½ Tbsps fish soy (nam pla)

3–4 Tbsps tamarind water (see page 12)

2 tsps sugar

Cut the fish into 1-inch (2-cm) chunks. Peel the daikon and cut it into ½ × ½ × 1½-inch (1 × 1 × 4-cm) strips. Cut the tomatoes into 1-inch (2-cm) chunks.

Put 6 cups of cold water in a medium-sized pot, bring to a boil over medium heat, and cook the daikon for 10–12 minutes. Add one-third of the fish and cook it with the daikon for 3 minutes.

Remove the fish only and whir it in a blender or food processor with the curry paste. Add this to the cooked daikon (in its cooking water) along with the tomatoes and the remaining two-thirds of the raw fish. Add all the SEASONINGS to the curry and mix well. Cook for 5–7 minutes, and serve hot with rice.

POULTRY

ไก่ — เป็ด

Chicken is so common that it is taken for granted in Thai cooking. It is enjoyed by rich and poor alike. In the countryside, the chicken seen scratching about the yard at noon may well be part of the evening meal.

Of course, chicken appears in curries. It is also barbecued or grilled and fried (without batter). With the latter two cooking methods, chicken is eaten with various dipping sauces (like the ones on pages 33-39), which bring out its natural flavor.

Duck comes from Chinese cooking and is eaten more in Thailand than in the West, but it is not nearly as common as chicken. Duck is largely used in curries. In the north of the country, pigeons and sparrows find their way into curries and are grilled and fried as well.

For whatever reason, maybe because chicken is taken so much for granted, classical Thai chicken dishes are delicious but not overly imaginative. There is thus a whole world of innovation possible in creating Thai *style* chicken dishes. We have exploited this potential a little in the recipes presented here.

♠ Green Curry with Chicken and Asparagus
(*Gang Keo Wan Gai*)

SERVES 6–8

1¾ lbs (800 gm) boneless dark chicken meat, cut into ¼ ×
    1 × 1½-inch (¾ × 2 × 4-cm) pieces
2 Tbsps white wine (or saké)
1 lb (450 gm) fresh asparagus
¼ cup coconut cream
3–4 Tbsps Green Curry Paste (see page 23)
3 cups coconut milk

1 cup coconut cream
7 fresh red chili peppers, seeded and cut lengthwise into 4–5 pieces
2–2½ Tbsps fish soy (*nam pla*)
sugar (optional)

GARNISH
¼ cup fresh sweet basil leaves

Marinate the chicken in the white wine (or saké) for 5 minutes.

Wash the asparagus and trim off the tough stem bottoms. Cut it on the diagonal into about 2-inch (5-cm) lengths.

Put ¼ cup of coconut cream in a medium-sized saucepan and heat it over medium heat. Stir the curry paste into the coconut cream and cook until the aroma is released—about 1 minute. Add the chicken and cook, stirring constantly, for 2 minutes. Add the asparagus and 3 cups of coconut milk. Boil gently for 5 minutes.

Add the final cup of coconut cream, the red chili peppers, and the fish soy. If desired, you can add 1–2 tsps of sugar to the curry.

Remove to a serving dish and sprinkle with fresh sweet basil leaves. Serve hot with rice.

♠ Nam Ya Curry with Chicken
(*Nam Ya Gai*)

Generally, nam ya *curries are soupy and gentle in flavor. They are often served with thin noodles (Kanom Chine, page 10).*

SERVES 6–8

5 cups coconut milk
1½ lbs (700 gm) chicken breast meat, cut into bite-sized chunks
3 Tbsps *Nam Ya* Curry Paste (see page 28)
2 Tbsps fish soy (*nam pla*)
1 cup coconut cream

GARNISHES
2 cups bean sprouts
5 mixed green and red chili peppers, seeded and cut lengthwise into fine slivers

1 cup dried (or fresh) lemon basil (*bai manglak*) leaves (optional)
3 hard-boiled eggs, peeled and quartered

Bring the 5 cups of coconut milk to a boil over medium heat in a saucepan. Add the chicken and cook for 5 minutes. Turn the heat off, remove the chicken from the coconut milk, and combine with the curry paste in a blender or food processor. Whir to form a rough paste. Return the chicken mixture to the coconut milk and bring to a boil over medium heat before adding the fish soy. Cook an additional 5 minutes and add the cup of coconut cream. Cover the pan and remove from the heat.

Prepare the GARNISHES. Pour boiling water over the cleaned bean sprouts, let sit for 1 minute, and plunge into cold water to refresh. Place each garnish in a serving dish.

Usually, this curry is served with very fine rice noodles (*Kanom Chine*, page 10), and the effect is not unlike western spaghetti and meat sauce. The GARNISHES are placed on top by each diner. The curry is also good with hot rice.

Variation
Substitute an equal amount of white-fleshed fish for the chicken.

▲ Baked Chicken and Mushrooms in Coconut Milk
(color page 15)

Oven cooking is not part of the Asian tradition. This dish is, of course, a blend of old and new Thailand.

SERVES 6–8

8 small boneless chicken breasts, skin removed
2 Tbsps vegetable oil
⅓ cup flour
3 cups coconut milk
3 Tbsps saké
2½ cups sliced button mushrooms (or any kind of mushroom)

1 tsp peppercorns, whole or freshly ground
1 Tbsp coarsely chopped garlic
2 tsps coarsely chopped coriander root

½ cup fish soy (*nam pla*)
1½ tsps sugar
2 tsps red pepper flakes

GARNISH
chopped parsley or green onion tops

Preheat oven to 350° F (175° C)

Place the 2 Tbsps oil in a frying pan over medium-high heat and brown the chicken breasts lightly. Set aside.

Blend the flour into the coconut milk and saké, then add the sliced mushrooms.

Pound the peppercorns, garlic, and coriander root to a paste in a mortar.

Mix the fish soy, sugar, and red pepper flakes.

Transfer the chicken breasts to a casserole. Blend together the coconut milk, garlic paste, and fish soy mixtures and pour the result over the chicken. Bake in a 350° F (175° C) oven for 40 minutes.

Sprinkle the chicken with chopped parsley or green onion and serve with rice or noodles.

▲ Steamed Chicken in Coconut Milk

This dish is attractive served double-plated in the French style, with crusty French bread or warm dinner rolls.

SERVES 6–8

8 small boneless chicken breasts, skin removed
¼ tsp salt
½ cup saké

SAUCE
4 cups coconut milk
1 Tbsp Red Curry Paste (see page 24)
1 tsp sugar
¼ tsp salt
2 tsps fish soy (*nam pla*)

GARNISH
chopped parsley or green onion tops

Clean all fat and skin from the chicken breasts. Sprinkle them with salt and marinate them in the saké for 15 minutes.

Heat a steamer (bamboo, preferably) and steam chicken breasts over medium heat for 15 minutes or until done.

While the chicken breasts are steaming, place all the SAUCE ingredients in a small pan and simmer over low heat for 3 minutes. The flavor is creamy coconut, salty, and slightly sweet.

Pour ½ cup of the coconut sauce into each warmed serving plate. Add one chicken breast to each plate and sprinkle with chopped parsley or chopped green onion tops.

♠ Chicken Drumsticks in Sour Curry

Serve this Thai-style original with German potato salad and garlic bread. Beer, too. Ideal picnic food.

SERVES 8–10

3 Tbsps vegetable oil
½ onion, julienned
8–10 chicken drumsticks
1 lb (450 gm) eggplant(s), western or Japanese
3–4 Tbsps Sour Curry Paste (see page 27)

5 medium tomatoes, peeled and quartered
1 green pepper, seeded and cut into ½ × 1½-inch (1 × 4-cm) pieces
1 cup cauliflower florets
2 stalks celery, cut into ½ × 1½-inch (1 × 4-cm) pieces
5 cups chicken stock (see page 11)
3 Tbsps fish soy (*nam pla*)
pinches of sugar and salt

Place oil in large frying pan or wok over medium heat. Fry the onion for 1 minute, then add the chicken drumsticks and brown them. Add the curry paste and thoroughly coat the drumsticks. Reduce heat to low and cook for 20–25 minutes.

Peel the eggplant(s) and cut into ½ × 1½-inch (1 × 4-cm) pieces. (Place in lightly vinegared water until ready to use to prevent discoloration.) Add all vegetables and the chicken stock to the drumsticks. Increase heat to medium and cook for 10 minutes. Be careful not to overcook the vegetables. Add the fish soy and sugar and adjust the flavor to taste.

Serve hot with rice.

♠ Stir-Fried Chicken with Red Curry
(*Pat Pet Gai*)

Like most other red curries, this is hot.

SERVES 6–8

1¾ lbs (800 gm) boneless chicken (white or dark meat or a combination)
2 Tbsps white wine (or saké)
4 Tbsps vegetable oil
3–4 Tbsps Red Curry Paste (see page 24)
10 oz (300 gm) green peppers, cut into 1 × 1½-inch (2 × 4-cm) pieces
2–2½ Tbsps fish soy (*nam pla*)
1 Tbsp sugar
7 fresh mixed green and red chili peppers, seeded and cut lengthwise
    into 4–5 pieces

1 Tbsp chopped fresh coriander leaves or ¼ cup fresh sweet basil

Cut the chicken into ¼ × 1 × 1½-inch (¾ × 2 × 4-cm) pieces. Marinate in the wine or saké for 5 minutes.

In a wok or large frying pan, heat the 4 Tbsps vegetable oil over medium heat and add the curry paste. Stir-fry until the aroma is released—a few seconds only. Add the chicken and stir-fry for 5–7 minutes. Add all the remaining ingredients (except the GARNISH). Stir-fry only 1–2 more minutes.

Place in a serving dish and sprinkle with coriander leaves or sweet basil. Serve hot as part of a Thai meal.

Variations
Since this is a basic Thai-style stir-fry recipe, you can substitute beef, pork, or fish with equally pleasant results. If the meat or fish is cut in pieces the same size as the chicken above, the cooking time remains the same. Fresh or frozen (not canned) green peas often take the place of the green peppers in this dish.

⚜ Thai Stewed Chicken

SERVES 6–8

2 3½-lb (1.5-kg) chickens
5 Tbsps Chinese sweet soy sauce (substitute 5 Tbsps regular
    soy sauce + 2½ Tbsps brown sugar)
2–3 stalks celery
8 dried shiitake mushrooms
10 slices fresh ginger
3–4 sprigs of fresh coriander
5–7 green onions

5 cups vegetable oil for deep-frying

½ tsp salt
3 Tbsps fish soy (*nam pla*)
2 tsps ground black pepper (or 10 peppercorns)
1 cup saké (or white cooking wine)

3 Tbsps cornstarch
3 Tbsps bean paste (Chinese or Japanese, but not the sweet type)

GARNISHES
6–8 fresh red chili peppers, cut into fine slivers
2 Tbsps chopped fresh coriander leaves

Wash the chickens and pat them dry inside and out. Rub them with the Chinese sweet soy sauce and let them sit for 30 minutes.

Prepare the vegetables and spices. Cut the celery into 3-inch (8-cm) pieces. Soak the dried mushrooms in warm water for 10 minutes, then trim off stems. Slice the ginger, and coarsely chop the coriander sprigs. Cut the green onions into 3-inch (8-cm) pieces.

Pour the 5 cups of vegetable oil into a very large wok and heat it to hot (360° F/180° C). Dry the chickens again (they must be absolutely dry, or the hot oil will spatter) and fry them until they turn a light yellow-brown color. It should take about 8 minutes for each side. Place the lightly fried chickens in a large stock pot and add 6 cups of water. Now add all the vegetables and seasonings—celery, soaked shiitake mushrooms, ginger slices, fresh coriander, green onions, salt, fish soy, pepper, and saké.

Cover the pot and boil the chickens over medium heat for 15 minutes. Turn the heat to low and simmer for 45 minutes. While the chickens are cooking, turn them 2–3 times to be sure the flavor is evenly distributed. The chickens should be very tender after 45 minutes—remove them and reduce the stock to 3 cups by boiling.

Add the cornstarch and bean paste to the stock, stirring constantly until the sauce thickens. Pour sauce over the whole chickens.

Sprinkle with coriander and slivers of chili. Carve the chickens at the table.

♠ Baked Chicken with Ginger Sauce

SERVES 6–8

2 3½-lb (1.5-kg) chickens

MARINADE
½ cup saké (or dry white wine)
2 cups vinegar
½ cup soy sauce
1 tsp pepper
3 Tbsps julienned ginger
1 Tbsp finely chopped coriander root

3 Tbsps flour
2 Tbsps vegetable oil

3 Tbsps cornstarch
1 Tbsp sesame oil

GARNISHES
3 green onions, finely chopped
2 Tbsps chopped fresh coriander leaves

Wash the chickens. Pat dry inside and out. Mix the marinade in a bowl large enough to hold both chickens. Add the chickens to the marinade, turn well to coat, and marinate for 5–6 hours at room temperature or overnight in the refrigerator. Turn chickens occasionally.

Heat the oven to 350° F (175° C). Remove the chickens from the MARINADE (reserve) and dredge them with the 3 Tbsps flour, then sprinkle with the 2 Tbsps of vegetable oil.

Place the chickens in a roaster and roast, uncovered, for 1 hour. Check to see if they are done—you may need an additional 15 minutes roasting time.

While the chickens are roasting, put the remaining marinade in a saucepan. There should be about 2 cups of liquid. Dissolve the 3 Tbsps cornstarch in the marinade and then bring it to a quick boil. Reduce the heat to low and cook for 5 minutes, stirring constantly. Add the Tbsp of sesame oil and taste the sauce—it should be sweet, sour, and salty.

Place the chickens on a serving platter and pour the hot sauce over them. Sprinkle with green onion and coriander leaves. Carve the chickens at the table.

▲ Chicken and Apple Curry

The Thai way of cooking this recipe is with bite-sized pieces of dark chicken meat. Substitute small drumsticks if you like, but first make a long slit down to the bone along each drumstick and open out the meat so the curry will penetrate fully.

SERVES 6–8

½ lb (225 gm) sour cooking apples

1⅓ lbs (600 gm) dark chicken meat, boned and cut into bite-sized pieces

3½ cups coconut milk

¼ cup coconut cream

3 Tbsps Red Curry Paste (page 24)

2–2½ Tbsps fish soy (*nam pla*)

1 tsp raw sugar

2 Tbsps tamarind water (see page 12)

GARNISHES

2 fresh kaffir lime leaves (*bai makrut*), cut into fine slivers (optional)

4–6 yellow or red chili peppers, cut into fine slivers

Peel the apples and cut them into ½ × 1½-inch (1 × 4-cm) chunks. Put in lightly salted water until ready to use to prevent discoloring.

Put the 3½ cups of coconut milk in a large saucepan over medium heat. Add the chicken, reduce heat to low, cover, and cook the chicken for 5 minutes. Drain the apples and add them to the pan. Cover and cook 5 more minutes.

While they are cooking, put the ¼ cup coconut cream in another pan over medium heat. Add the curry paste and cook until the aroma is released—about 1 minute.

Add this to the chicken and apples along with the fish soy, sugar, and tamarind water. Cook over low heat for 5 minutes.

Place in a serving dish and sprinkle with kaffir lime leaf slivers and chili pepper slivers before serving.

Western Variation
Reduce the coconut milk and curry paste to half the amounts called for. All other ingredients and the cooking method are the same. Serve with mashed potatoes rather than rice.

♠ Barbecued Chicken, Thai Style
(color page 17)

This hot barbecued chicken and the cold Sweet Pork (see page 142) make the basis of an excellent picnic.

SERVES 4–6

4 lbs (about 2 kg) chicken fryer pieces

SEASONINGS
3 Tbsps coarsely chopped garlic
2 tsps coarsely chopped coriander root (substitute 1 tsp ground coriander seed)
1 tsp powdered turmeric
3 fresh (or dried) red chili peppers, seeded (soaked, if dried)
    and coarsely chopped
1 tsp curry powder
1 Tbsp sugar
¼ tsp salt

3 Tbsps fish soy (*nam pla*)

¼ cup coconut milk

Clean the chicken pieces; wash and pat dry.

Combine the SEASONINGS in a blender or food processor and make a coarse paste. Place the paste in a large mixing bowl, add the fish soy, and mix thoroughly. Add the chicken and mix well with your hands. Marinate in the refrigerator overnight or at least 2 hours at room temperature.

Arrange the chicken pieces on a barbecue grill (or in a broiler) and brush evenly with the coconut milk. Barbecue or broil till done and serve with the BARBECUE CHICKEN SAUCE and steamed glutinous rice.

BARBECUE CHICKEN SAUCE
2 dried red chili peppers, seeded, soaked, and coarsely chopped
2 cloves garlic, coarsely chopped

1 Tbsp raw sugar

¼ tsp salt

½ cup rice vinegar

GARNISHES

a few fresh coriander leaves

1–2 green onions, finely chopped

In a blender, food processor, or mortar, make a paste from the first four ingredients. Mix in the vinegar and place in a serving dish. Sprinkle with fresh coriander and green onion.

♠ Chicken with Green Curry

This dish is designed for busy people. The usual lengthy chopping has been eliminated, and the result is almost French. This goes well with buttered artichoke hearts or okra.

SERVES 8

8 boneless chicken breasts, skin removed

2½ Tbsps white wine

pinch of salt

SAUCE

2½ cups coconut milk

2–3 Tbsps Green Curry Paste (see page 23)

1 Tbsp fish soy (*nam pla*)

another pinch of salt

½ tsp sugar

2 oz (60 gm) spinach, stems removed

Wash the chicken breasts and trim off any fat. Flatten them by pounding lightly, then marinate in the wine and salt for 15 minutes.

Place the chicken breasts in a steamer and steam for 7 minutes. Turn the heat off and leave the breasts in the covered steamer for 5 minutes.

While the chicken is steaming, make the SAUCE. Place the coconut milk in a saucepan and add the curry paste, fish soy, salt, and sugar.

Blanch the spinach in ample boiling water, plunge into cold water, and gently squeeze all the water out. Puree the spinach in a blender or food processor.

Add the spinach to the coconut milk mixture and bring to a boil over medium heat. Adjust seasoning to taste—it should be salty and peppery.

Warm 8 serving plates. Place a chicken breast on each one and spoon ¼ cup sauce around it.

Serve warm with rice, noodles, or mashed potatoes.

♠ Duck and Pineapple Curry

2 Tbsps vegetable oil

1½ lbs (700 gm) boned duck meat, skin and fat removed and cut into thin, bite-sized pieces

¼ cup coconut cream

2–3 Tbsps Red Curry Paste (see page 24)

½ small pineapple, peeled, cored, and cut into small chunks

4 cups coconut milk

3 Tbsps fish soy (*nam pla*)

2 tsps raw sugar

1 Tbsp lime (or lemon) juice

Garnishes

chopped fresh coriander leaves

fresh red chili peppers, cut into fine slivers

Place oil in a wok or frying pan over medium-high heat. When hot, add duck and stir-fry until well cooked—about 3–4 minutes. Set aside.

Place ¼ cup coconut cream in a saucepan over medium heat and add the curry paste. Simmer until aroma is released—about 1 minute. Add pineapple chunks, duck, and coconut milk, reduce heat to low, and simmer, stirring frequently, until duck is tender (about 10–12 minutes).

Add fish soy, sugar, and lime juice and adjust seasonings to taste.

Place in a serving dish and garnish with coriander leaves and red chili pepper slivers.

Serve hot. Excellent with noodles.

Variation

Very young onions and small turnips go well in this dish. Add either or both with the coconut milk.

MEAT

เนื้อ

The Thai people eat a wide variety of meat. This might surprise those who know that Buddhism is a state religion and that about 98 percent of the Thai people claim to be Buddhists. In the villages, religion is bound up with every aspect of daily life.

How do devout Buddhists, who may not harm even a fly, justify eating every kind of meat available? The answer is simple—they do not kill any animal. There are several thousand Chinese butchers happy to oblige. And, of course, the pragmatic Thais would not let anything go to waste. They make wonderful meat dishes.

Many of the recipes in this book call for marinating meat in red or white wine or saké. This, of course, is borrowed from western and Chinese cooking. Wine or saké marination improves the flavor of meat, especially pork and beef. Marination is our addition, and readers may wish to omit it for "authenticity's" sake.

♠ Green Curry with Pork and Green Tomatoes

SERVES 6–8

2 lbs (1 kg) thinly sliced pork shoulder (or whatever cut you like)

10 oz (300 gm) green tomatoes

¼ cup coconut cream

3–4 Tbsps Green Curry Paste (see page 23)

3 cups coconut milk

1 additional cup coconut cream

2–2½ Tbsps fish soy (*nam pla*)

2 tsps sugar

7 mixed red and green chili peppers, sliced lengthwise into 4–5 pieces

GARNISH

¼ cup fresh sweet basil leaves

Cut the thinly sliced pork into 1 × 1½-inch (2 × 4-cm) pieces. Cut the green tomatoes into 1-inch (2-cm) chunks.

Put the ¼ cup of coconut cream in a medium-sized saucepan over medium heat. Add the curry paste and cook until the aroma is released— about 1 minute. Add the pork and cook for 5 minutes. Add the green tomatoes, coconut milk, additional cup of coconut cream, fish soy, and sugar. Add the sliced chili peppers. When heated through, transfer to a serving dish and sprinkle with fresh sweet basil. Serve hot with rice or noodles.

♠ Pork, Chicken, and Egg Stew
(*Tom Kem*)

This stew can be prepared up to a week ahead and tastes better after the second day. Excellent for a buffet, a hearty dinner, or a picnic. In Thailand this is always one of the noncurry dishes in the shiny pots at rural food stalls.

SERVES 12

SEASONINGS

2 Tbsps coarsely chopped coriander root

2 Tbsps coarsely chopped garlic

1 Tbsp peppercorns, whole or freshly ground

3 red chili peppers (fresh or dried; optional)

3 Tbsps vegetable oil

¾ cup raw sugar

½ cup soy sauce

½ cup fish soy (*nam pla*)

½ cup saké

10 hard-boiled eggs, peeled

2½ lbs (1.2 kg) chicken pieces (drumsticks, thighs, and wings)

2½ lbs (1.2 kg) pork (any cut), cut into 2-inch (5-cm) chunks
6 dried shiitake mushrooms, soaked, stems removed, and cut into 1-inch (2-cm) pieces
3 lbs (1.5 kg) thick deep-fried tofu (Japanese: *nama-age*; or use regular tofu)

3 Tbsps oil

GARNISH
chopped fresh coriander leaves or slivered green onions

Pound the coriander root, garlic, peppercorns, and chili to a paste in a mortar.

Place the 3 Tbsps of oil in a large pot over medium heat. Add the paste and stir-fry until the aroma is released—a few seconds only. Add the remaining SEASONINGS. Stir well and add the saké and 2 cups water.

Add the whole eggs to the simmering broth in the pot along with the chicken, pork, mushrooms, and tofu.

The liquid should be a coffee-brown color. If it is not, add more raw sugar and soy sauce. Simmer, stirring occasionally, 45–50 minutes or until the chicken and pork are tender.

Garnish with chopped coriander leaves or chopped green onions and serve with rice.

♠ Stir-Fried Pork with Daikon Radish

Dried shaved daikon (Japanese: kiriboshi daikon) is becoming increasingly available in the United States. If this ingredient is elusive, substitute julienned fresh daikon. Icicle radishes, turnips, rutabaga, and kohlrabi are also good prepared this way.

SERVES 6

3 Tbsps vegetable oil
1 Tbsp finely chopped garlic
1 cup julienned lean pork (or leftover roast pork)
2 cups dried daikon radish shavings (Japanese: *kiriboshi daikon*)

SEASONINGS
2 Tbsps fish soy (*nam pla*)
1 tsp sugar
½ tsp black pepper

3 eggs, well beaten

GARNISH
1 Tbsp chopped fresh coriander leaves or slivered green onion tops

Heat the 3 Tbsps vegetable oil in a frying pan or wok over medium heat and stir-fry the garlic until it just turns color. Add the pork and daikon and stir-fry the mixture for 5 minutes. Add the SEASONINGS and stir-fry 1 minute more. Pour the beaten egg over the frying mixture and cook, stirring 5–6 times, until set.

Mound the mixture decoratively on lettuce on a serving dish or on individual plates. Sprinkle with coriander or green onion tops. Serve hot.

Variation
For a vegetarian dish or just a change of pace, substitute ½ lb (225 gm) of mashed tofu for the pork. Break it up with a spatula while frying.

▲ Red Curry with Pork and Eggplant
(*Gang Pet Mu*)

This classic Thai dish is HOT. Cut down the amount of chili pepper and red curry paste if you are cooking for palates unaccustomed to fire.

SERVES 6–8

1½ lbs (700 gm) thinly sliced pork shoulder (or the cut of your choice)
1 lb (450 gm) eggplant(s)
¼ cup coconut cream
3 Tbsps Red Curry Paste (see page 24)
4 cups coconut milk
2 Tbsps fish soy (*nam pla*)
½ tsp sugar
5–7 mixed fresh red and green chili peppers, seeded and
    cut lengthwise into 4–5 pieces
1 kaffir lime leaf (*bai makrut*), cut into fine slivers (optional)

GARNISH
¼ cup fresh sweet basil leaves

Cut the thinly sliced pork into 1 × 1½-inch (2 × 4-cm) pieces. Cut the eggplant(s) into 1-inch (2-cm) chunks and immediately put into lightly salted water to prevent discoloration.

Put the ¼ cup of coconut cream in a saucepan over medium heat. Mix in the curry paste and cook until the aroma is released—about 1 minute. Add the pork and cook 5 minutes. Add the 4 cups of coconut milk, the eggplant, the fish soy, sugar, chili peppers, and the kaffir lime leaf and cook 3–4 minutes.

Place in a serving dish and sprinkle with fresh sweet basil. Serve hot with rice.

Variations
This is an extremely common Thai curry, and, as such, the variations and options in preparation are many.

If you do not like it this mild, obviously you can add more curry paste. If you do not like it this hot, adding some green pepper strips or chunks will decrease the bite. If you do not like the curry this soupy, simply decrease the coconut milk. (The coconut cream amount should be the same.) Finally, if you do not want to use pork, an equal amount of firm white-fleshed fish is wonderful in this recipe.

♠ Spicy Roast Pork with Pineapple

East meets West. Serve this spicy roast pork with mashed potatoes sprinkled with toasted sesame seeds. Accompany with a simple green salad.

SERVES 6–8

4–5 lbs (2 kg) pork roast

SEASONINGS
2–2½ Tbsps Peppery Curry Paste (see page 28)
2½ Tbsps soy sauce
1 tsp sugar
2 tsps vinegar

2 Tbsps vegetable oil
2 Tbsps flour

2–3 onions, quartered
1 pineapple, peeled, cored, and cut lengthwise into 8 spears

GARNISH
16 cherry tomatoes

Wash the roast and pat it dry. Blend the SEASONINGS ingredients and rub the paste on the pork. Sprinkle the 2 Tbsps of vegetable oil over the meat and then dredge with flour.

Place in a roasting pan and roast at 300° F (150° C) for 1½ hours. Increase the heat to 375° F (190° C), place the pineapple spears and onions around the roast, and bake for 20 more minutes.

Remove the meat to a warm platter and decoratively arrange the pineapple spears and cherry tomatoes around it, adding a touch of green if you like. Carve the meat at the table.

♠ Stir-Fried Pork and Green Beans
(*Pat Prik King*)

Beef or chicken can be used with equal success in this recipe. If you are fortunate enough to have any left over, this dry curry is wonderful heated and used as a hot sandwich filling. Brown breads—wheat or rye—seem to be the best for spicy curry sandwiches.

SERVES 6–8

1 lb (450 gm) very thinly sliced (sukiyaki style) pork (any cut)

⅓ cup vegetable oil
2–2½ Tbsps Peppery Curry Paste (see page 28)
3 oz (90 gm) dried shrimp, rinsed
¼ lb (115 gm) green beans, cut diagonally into 1½-inch (4-cm) pieces
2 oz (60 gm) peanuts, coarsely chopped or crushed
1 tsp sugar

2 Tbsps fish soy (*nam pla*)

GARNISH

**2 fresh kaffir lime leaves (*bai makrut*), cut into fine slivers
(substitute 6–8 fresh sweet basil leaves)**

Wash the pork and cut it into 1 × 1½-inch (2 × 4-cm) pieces.

Add the oil to a wok or frying pan over medium heat. Add the curry paste and stir-fry until the aroma is released—a few seconds only.

Add the pork and stir-fry 3 minutes; add the dried shrimp and stir-fry for 3 more minutes. Add the green beans, peanuts, sugar, and fish soy. Stir-fry a final 3 minutes.

Place in a serving dish and sprinkle with kaffir lime leaf slivers (or sweet basil leaves). Serve hot.

▲ Stir-fried Pork with Mixed Vegetables

Almost any combination of vegetables, cooked or raw, can be used in this recipe. Cooking time will vary somewhat, depending on the ingredients. It is easy to judge. Vegetarians can simply omit the pork.

SERVES 6–8

½ lb (225 gm) thinly sliced pork shoulder (or your favorite cut)

MARINADE

1 tsp ginger juice (see page 10)
2 tsps saké
pinch of salt

¼ lb (115 gm) canned baby corn
¼ lb (115 gm) button mushrooms
¼ lb (115 gm) fresh asparagus
2 oz (60 gm) cooked (or canned) bamboo shoots
2 oz (60 gm) snow peas
3–4 green onions
½ medium carrot

⅓ cup vegetable oil
2 cloves garlic, coarsely chopped
2 Tbsps cornstarch dissolved in ½ cup water
½ tsp pepper
½ tsp salt
2 Tbsps fish soy (*nam pla*)
1 Tbsp sesame oil

Cut the thinly sliced pork into 1 × 1½-inch (2 × 4-cm) pieces. Marinate the pork in the ginger juice, saké, and salt for 5 minutes.

Prepare all the vegetables. Leave the baby corn whole; cut the mushrooms in half; trim off the tough parts of the asparagus and cut diagonally into 1½-inch (4-cm) lengths; cut the bamboo shoots into ½ × 1½-inch (1 × 4-cm) pieces; string the snow peas and leave them whole; cut the green onions (including the tops) into 1½-inch (4-cm) lengths; and cut the carrot to match the bamboo shoots.

Set a wok over high heat, heat the oil, and stir-fry the garlic until it changes color. Add the pork and stir-fry over high heat for 2–3 minutes. Remove and reserve the pork and garlic but leave the oil.

Add the baby corn, mushrooms, asparagus, bamboo shoots, and 3 Tbsps water. Stir-fry for 2 minutes. Add the remaining vegetables, the pork and garlic, cornstarch-water mixture, pepper, salt, fish soy, and sesame oil. Stir-fry 2 more minutes. Serve hot.

♠ Pork Fried with Garlic and Black Pepper

One of the simplest of all Thai dishes, this one is also extremely common. The secret is to use lots of garlic. Thai black pepper is slightly different from western black pepper and is very good in this. Fresh pig's or calf's liver, cut the same way, is often substituted in Thailand.

SERVES 6

1 lb (450 gm) thinly sliced pork (any cut)

3 Tbsps vegetable oil

4 Tbsps coarsely chopped garlic

1 tsp coarsely chopped coriander root (optional)

2 Tbsps fish soy (*nam pla*)

½ tsp freshly ground black pepper

Cut the thinly sliced pork into 1 × 2-inch (2 × 5-cm) pieces.

Add the vegetable oil to a wok or large frying pan over high heat. Stir-fry the garlic just until it starts to change color. Add the coriander root and pork. Stir-fry over high heat for 3–5 minutes or until the pork is no longer pink. Add the fish soy and black pepper and stir-fry for 1 more minute.

Serve hot with rice as part of a Thai meal.

♠ Sweet Pork

There are two methods for cooking this: one is to cut the meat into thin pieces and the other is to keep the pork in a single piece. As an hors d'oeuvre or as part of a buffet, it is better to cut the meat. As a main course, it is better to leave the meat in one piece. This keeps well when refrigerated and is also good for hikers and campers. It travels well.

SERVES 6

2 lbs (1 kg) pork shoulder

1½ Tbsps saké

2 Tbsps coarsely chopped garlic

10–12 peppercorns, whole or freshly ground

3 coriander roots, coarsely chopped

2 Tbsps fish soy (*nam pla*)

pinch of salt

2½ Tbsps raw sugar

½ cup thinly sliced onion

¼ cup vegetable oil

GARNISH

chopped fresh coriander leaves

If you are using the sweet pork as part of a buffet or as an hors d'oeuvre, have the butcher slice the meat very thin (sukiyaki style) and cut it into 1 × 2-inch (2 × 5-cm) pieces. If you intend to serve it as the main course, leave the meat in one piece.

Marinate the meat in the saké for 10 minutes.

Whir the garlic, peppercorns, coriander roots, fish soy, salt, and sugar in a blender or food processor to a fine paste.

In a Dutch oven or large frying pan with a lid, heat the ½ cup of vegetable oil to medium hot. Add the onions, fry them until they turn golden, and remove them from the oil. Add the paste made from the garlic and other ingredients and stir-fry it until the aroma is released—a few seconds only. Add the sliced meat and stir-fry it over medium heat for 5–7 minutes. Add ½ cup of water, reduce the heat to low, cover, and simmer for 20 minutes or until the meat is tender and the liquid has evaporated (a dry sauce without juice). If the sauce is not completely dry, remove the cover and cook the meat until the liquid evaporates.

If you are using a block of meat, sauté each side for 3 minutes after stir-frying the paste. Add the ½ cup of water, cover, reduce the heat to low, and simmer for 30 to 40 minutes or until the meat is tender. Remove to a serving platter, pour on the remaining sauce, and sprinkle the pork with fresh coriander leaves. Slice it at the table.

▲ Spicy Meat in Raw Cabbage Leaves

Any leftover meat (even turkey) can be ground and cooked this way. This dish can also be a great sandwich spread. A simple yoghurt soup would be a welcome complement for a summer lunch.

SERVES 6

1 lb (450 gm) lean ground pork, beef, or chicken breast meat

½ cup thinly sliced red onions, coarsely chopped

¼ cup fresh mint, chopped

1½ Tbsps finely chopped fresh lemon grass (or 3 Tbsps dried)

2–2½ Tbsps fish soy (*nam pla*)

juice of ½ lemon (or lime)

4–6 guinea peppers (*prik kee nu*) (substitute 2 tsps red pepper flakes)

GARNISHES

½ cup crushed parched rice (see page 119; substitute Grape Nuts)

2 green onions, finely chopped

1 Tbsp chopped fresh coriander leaves

12–18 cabbage leaves

Bring 2 cups of water to a boil in a saucepan. Add the meat, break it up with a fork, and bring the water to a boil again over high heat. Immediately when the water starts to boil, drain the meat and cool it—the meat should still be slightly pink. Let the meat cool to room temperature. If you refrigerate it, the fat will coagulate.

Add the onion, mint, and lemon grass to the meat along with the fish soy, lemon (or lime) juice, and guinea peppers. Mix thoroughly and taste—it should be salty, hot, and sour.

Prepare the parched rice. Sprinkle it over the meat with the green onion and fresh coriander leaves.

Serve with the tender cabbage leaves from the center of the head. To eat, spoon some of the meat on top of a cabbage leaf and eat with your fingers.

♠ Red Curry with Beef and Bamboo Shoots
(*Gang Pet Nya*)

This hot curry is very popular in Thailand because it goes well with boiled rice. Adapt it and tone it down as you like.

SERVES 6–8

1½ lbs (700 gm) thinly sliced beef (rump roast is suitable)

1 lb (450 gm) cooked (or canned) bamboo shoots, thinly sliced

4 cups coconut milk

¼ cup coconut cream

3½ Tbsps Red Curry Paste (see page 24)

5 fresh mixed green and red chili peppers, cut into 4–5 pieces lengthwise

2 Tbsps fish soy (*nam pla*)

sugar (optional)

Wash the beef and cut it into 1 × 1½-inch (2 × 4-cm) pieces. Cut the bamboo shoots the same size.

If using an inexpensive cut of beef, tenderize it by gently boiling for 15 minutes in the 4 cups of coconut milk. If using good beef, simply cook the beef in the 4 cups of coconut milk for 5 minutes.

Put the ¼ cup of coconut cream in a separate saucepan over medium heat, mix in the curry paste, and cook until the aroma is released—about 1 minute. Add the bamboo shoots and then add this mixture to the cooked beef. Add the chili peppers and the fish soy to the curry. Mix well. If you like, mix in a small amount of sugar at this time. Heat the curry through and serve with rice or noodles.

Variations
Instead of bamboo shoots, use an equal amount of cut green beans, zucchini, or winter squash. Boned chicken, the same weight as the beef and cut into ½-inch (1-cm) chunks, can be used instead of beef.

▲ Stir-Fried Beef with Tofu and Mushrooms

SERVES 6–8

2 lbs (1 kg) regular tofu (Japanese "cotton" tofu; the deep-fried type known as *nama age* in Japanese is excellent for this)
10 oz (300 gm) inexpensive, very thinly sliced (sukiyaki style) beef

MARINADE
2 Tbsps saké
1 Tbsp cornstarch
2 Tbsps soy sauce

1 cup dried shiitake mushrooms, reconstituted in warm water for 30 minutes (3.0 oz) 2 pack.
½ cup vegetable oil   = 2 cups
1 Tbsp crushed garlic

SEASONINGS   (1.5 oz) 1 pack
2 Tbsps soy sauce   = 1 cup
½ tsp pepper   (not what package says)
1 tsp sugar
3–4 fresh chili peppers, seeded and cut lengthwise into 4–5 pieces or 1 tsp red pepper powder
3–4 green onions, cut into 1½-inch (4-cm) lengths or cut 5 mms .+ 6 dashes hot oil (chilies)

If using regular tofu, wrap it in a kitchen towel, weight with 2 dinner plates, and drain for 20 minutes. Cut tofu into ½ × ½ × 1½-inch (1 × 1 × 4-cm) pieces.

Cut the thinly sliced beef into 1 × 2-inch (2 × 5-cm) pieces and marinate it in the saké, cornstarch, and soy sauce for 5 minutes.

Trim off the mushroom stems and cut the mushroom caps into quarters.

Heat the ½ cup of vegetable oil in a wok over high heat. Fry the tofu until it begins to change color. Turn it over, being careful not to break the pieces, and again fry until color changes. (*Nama age* requires less cooking time.) Remove the tofu but leave the oil in the wok. Add the garlic and stir-fry until it begins to brown. Add the mushrooms and stir-fry for 1–2 minutes, add the sukiyaki beef and MARINADE and stir-fry an additional 2 minutes. Return the tofu to the pan and add all the SEASONINGS plus ¼ cup water. Stir-fry 5 minutes. Add the green onion and cook only 15 seconds. Serve hot.

Vegetarian Variation
The beef is not an essential part of this recipe. The shiitake mushrooms and tofu are delicious by themselves.

♠ Chuck Roast with Sour Curry
(color page 16)

This is a dish for hearty meat eaters and probably one of the best examples in this book of the fusion of Thai and western cooking.

SERVES 6–8

3 lbs (1½ kg) chuck roast

VEGETABLES
1 medium carrot, cut into ½ × ½ × 1½-inch (1 × 1 × 4-cm) pieces
2 stalks celery, cut into ½ × ½ × 1½-inch (1 × 1 × 4-cm) pieces
1 onion, halved lengthwise, then cut into ½-inch (1-cm) pieces crosswise
1 green pepper, cut into 1½-inch (4-cm) pieces
1 medium tomato, peeled and cut into 6–8 wedges

3 Tbsps vegetable oil
3 Tbsps flour
4 Tbsps Sour Curry Paste (see page 27)
2 cups stock (from cooking roast)
⅓ cup fish soy (*nam pla*)
juice of ¼ lemon

GARNISHES
chopped green onions
chopped fresh coriander leaves
red chili peppers, cut into fine slivers

Wash the chuck roast and place in a large pot with 6 cups of cold water. Bring to a boil and cook over medium heat for 30 minutes. While meat is cooking, prepare the VEGETABLES. Add them to the roast and cook 20 minutes more.

Remove the meat and vegetables and strain the stock, saving 2 cups.

Put the 3 Tbsps vegetable oil in a frying pan over medium heat. Add the 3 Tbsps flour and make a smooth paste. Add the Sour Curry Paste and reserved 2 cups of stock. Blend well and add the fish soy and lemon juice.

Arrange the meat on a platter. Either slice it in the kitchen or at the table. Pour the seasoned gravy over the meat and arrange the vegetables around it. Sprinkle with chopped green onion, coriander, and red chili slivers to taste. Serve hot.

♠ Masaman Curry with Beef

(*Gang Masaman Nya*)
(color pages 18–19)

Of the hundreds of Thai curries, this one is extremely popular with westerners. It makes a fine main dish in a western meal, served with noodles or rice and a simple vegetable.

SERVES 6–8

4 Tbsps vegetable oil
1 cup julienned onions
3–4 Tbsps *Masaman* Curry Paste (see page 23)
3⅓ lbs (1.5 kg) stewing beef, cut into 1½-inch (4-cm) chunks
4 cups coconut milk
1 lb (450 gm) potatoes, peeled and cut into 1½-inch (4-cm) chunks
1 cup coarsely chopped or crushed peanuts
¼ cup tamarind water (see page 12)
1–2 Tbsps sugar
3½ Tbsps fish soy (*nam pla*)

Heat the 4 Tbsps vegetable oil in a large frying pan or wok and add the julienned onions. Fry over medium heat until golden and remove from the oil. Add the curry paste and fry it over low heat for 2 minutes. Add the meat and 4 cups of coconut milk and cook for 25 minutes or until the meat is tender. Add the potatoes to the beef along with all remaining ingredients including the fried onions. Cook over low heat until potatoes are done—15–20 minutes.

Place in a serving dish and serve hot with rice, hot Japanese *somen* noodles, or any kind of fine pasta.

Variation
Substitute an equal amount of chicken for the beef chunks. Cooking time will be the same.

♠ Green Curry with Beef

(*Gang Keo Wan Nya*)

This dish is the Thai equivalent of green chili—the curry paste is made with green chili peppers, and a fresh green vegetable is included. Commercial green curry paste packaged in jars and plastic does not have the fresh flavor of that made at home.

SERVES 6–8

1¾ lbs (800 gm) thinly sliced beef (chuck or rump roast)
1¼ cups coconut cream
3–4 Tbsps Green Curry Paste (see page 23)
10 oz (300 gm) green beans, snapped into 1½-inch (4-cm) lengths

3 cups coconut milk

2–2½ Tbsps fish soy (*nam pla*)

2 tsps sugar

7 fresh red chili peppers, cut lengthwise into 4–5 pieces

<small>GARNISH</small>

¼ cup fresh sweet basil leaves

Cut the thinly sliced beef into 1 × 1½-inch (2 × 4-cm) pieces. Heat ¼ cup of the coconut cream in a saucepan over medium heat. Add the curry paste and mix until the aroma is released—about 1 minute. Add the beef and cook 8 minutes. Add the green beans, the remaining coconut cream, the 3 cups of coconut milk, the fish soy, sugar, and fresh red chili peppers. Cook for 4–5 minutes.

Place in a serving dish and sprinkle with fresh sweet basil leaves. As with most Thai curries, this is best with hot rice.

▲ Panang Curry with Beef
(*Panang Nya*)

Author Mike Worman reminisces, "I once was discussing Thai food with twin teenage Thai girls studying in Tokyo. 'What is really your absolutely favorite Thai food?' one of them asked. Without much hesitation I replied, 'Panang Nya.' But Panang Nya *doesn't count, protested the other twin. If there's anyone living who doesn't love* Panang Nya, *they would just have to be crazy.' "*

SERVES 6–8

2 lbs (1 kg) beef chuck or rump roast

<small>MARINADE</small>

1 Tbsp fish soy (*nam pla*)

1 Tbsp red wine

2 cups coconut milk

¼ cup coconut cream

2½–3 Tbsps *Panang* Curry Paste (see page 29)

2 Tbsps fish soy (*nam pla*)

2 tsps raw sugar

**5 mixed fresh green and red chili peppers, seeded and cut
    lengthwise into 4–5 pieces**

<small>GARNISH</small>

**1 fresh kaffir lime leaf (*bai makrut*), cut into fine slivers
    (substitute 6–8 sweet basil leaves)**

Cut the meat into very thin bite-sized pieces. If the meat is slightly frozen it will be easier to slice thinly. Marinate the cut meat in 1 Tbsp fish soy and 1 Tbsp red wine for 10 minutes.

Place the 2 cups of coconut milk in a saucepan and bring it barely to a boil. Add the marinated meat and cook for 15 minutes or until the meat is tender.

Place the ¼ cup of coconut cream in a frying pan over medium heat and mix in the curry paste. Stir until the curry releases its aroma—about 1 minute. Pour this mixture over the meat.

Mix in the 2 Tbsps fish soy, sugar, and chili peppers. Heat through.

Place in a serving dish and sprinkle with the kaffir lime leaf (or sweet basil). Dry and delicious, this is always served with rice.

♠ Gang Ba (Country Style) Curry with Chuck Roast
(*Gang Ba Nya*)

Traditionally this country style curry is made with whatever you have in the house. As mentioned elsewhere, the pastes are made up in large amounts and stored in earthen jars. Then whatever meat, fish, and vegetables are in the kitchen are combined to make this simple but substantial curry. The slightly sour tang of the gang ba curry paste goes well with beef, not unlike German sauerbraten.

In poor Thai country homes, this curry is made with vegetables only, with delicious results.

SERVES 6–8

**1¾ lbs (800 gm) very thinly sliced (sukiyaki style) beef
    (chuck or rump roast)**
10 oz (300 gm) eggplant (substitute potato or bamboo shoots)

½ cup vegetable oil
3 Tbsps *Gang Ba* Curry Paste (see page 27)
7 mixed fresh green and red chili peppers, cut lengthwise into 4–5 pieces
2½ Tbsps fish soy (*nam pla*)
1 fresh (or dried) kaffir lime leaf (*bai makrut*), torn into 2–3 pieces
1 tsp raw sugar
2 Tbsps holy basil leaves (*bai krapau*)

Cut the beef slices into ½ × 1½-inch (1 × 4-cm) pieces. Cut the eggplant (or potatoes or bamboo shoots) into ½ × 1-inch (1 × 2-cm) chunks.

Put the ½ cup of vegetable oil in a wok or frying pan over medium-high heat. Add the curry paste and stir-fry until the aroma is released—a few seconds only. Add 4 cups of water and the beef and cook for 8–10 minutes. Add the eggplant, chili, fish soy, the kaffir lime leaf, and the sugar. Cook for 5–8 minutes. Just before removing from the pan, add the 2 Tbsps of holy basil. Serve hot with rice.

♨ Beef with Oyster Sauce
(Nya Pat Naman Hoy)

Probably the only thing separating this Thai dish from its Chinese cousin is the addition of the red chili peppers, and even that is not foreign to China. To westernize this dish, leave the beef in whole fillets, each about ¼ lb (100 gm). The cooking time is the same—the beef fillets will cook quickly.

SERVES 6–8

1⅓ lbs (600 gm) high-quality beef fillet, thinly sliced
dash of pepper
1 Tbsp saké (or red wine)
2 tsps cornstarch
pinch salt and pepper
¼ cup vegetable oil
2–3 cloves garlic, coarsely chopped

SEASONINGS
3 Tbsps oyster sauce
1½ Tbsps soy sauce
1 Tbsp honey
1 Tbsp lemon juice
3 slices fresh ginger

4–5 fresh or dried red chili peppers, cut in half lengthwise
3 green onions, cut in 1½-inch (4-cm) lengths

GARNISH
2–3 lettuce leaves, roughly torn

Cut the sliced beef into 1 × 1½-inch (2 × 4-cm) pieces. Marinate it for 10 minutes in the saké (or wine), cornstarch, salt, and pepper.

Heat the oil in a wok over high heat. Add the garlic and stir-fry just until the color changes, then add the beef. Stir-fry 30 seconds only, add the SEASONINGS all at once and stir-fry for 3 minutes.

Add the chili peppers and green onion and stir-fry 1 final minute. Arrange the lettuce leaves on a serving platter and place the beef on top. Sprinkle with a dash of black pepper and serve.

♨ Red Curry with Beef and Green Peppers
(Phra Ram Dern Daeng)

SERVES 6–8

1 lb (450 gm) thinly sliced choice chuck blade steak
4 Tbsps vegetable oil
1–1½ Tbsps Red Curry Paste (see page 24)

¼ lb (115 gm) green peppers, seeded

1 tsp sugar

Garnishes

2 Tbsps coarsely torn holy basil (*bai krapau*; optional)

2 fresh kaffir lime leaves (*bai makrut*), roughly torn (optional)

red pepper flakes (optional)

Wash the meat and cut it into 1 × 1½-inch (2 × 4-cm) pieces. Slice the green peppers into thin, 2-inch (5-cm) long strips.

Heat the vegetable oil in a wok or frying pan over high heat until it is almost smoking. Add the curry paste and stir-fry until the aroma is released—a few seconds. Immediately add the meat and stir-fry over high heat for 3 minutes. Add the green pepper, fish soy, and sugar, and stir-fry 3 more minutes.

Place in a serving dish and sprinkle with the holy basil and kaffir lime leaves (and red pepper flakes, if you like). Serve hot with rice.

Variations

Replace the green peppers with thinly sliced daikon radish or bamboo shoots.

RICE, NOODLES

ข้าว — หมี่

To the Thai people, rice is FOOD. It is the staple that appears at every meal. It is the reminder that there is enough to eat and that all is well (as in the words of the song quoted on page 109).

Thais always make more plain boiled rice than is needed for one meal. This is so that one of the numerous fried rice dishes can be made with the leftover cooked rice. These dishes use almost all the leftovers on hand—pork, chicken, green peas, eggs, seafood, whatever. Form the simplest roadside stand to the most sumptuous outdoor seafood restaurant—all serve fried rice. Knowledgable visitors, young foreigners traveling on a shoestring, American military men, and Peace Corps volunteers seem to agree that one has to make a very big effort indeed to find bad fried rice in Thailand. And the variations are endless. Once you start to experiment, you can create a masterpiece.

Asian noodles remain an unexplored territory for the West. Mung bean noodles, egg noodles, rice noodles, buckwheat noodles, tea noodles; thin, thick, flat, square, straight, curly; hand stretched, hand cut—one has a lot to be confused by. There are so many kinds in so many countries. Depending on the national origin of your advisor (friend, teacher, shopkeeper), the noodle changes its name. The simple mung bean noodle has at least fifteen names, depending on who is talking about it.

Thailand, naturally, has its noodles—both wham-slam dishes and fussy extravaganzas. In many cases, Thai noodle dishes are indistinguishable from their Chinese counterparts. Two—the wonderful sweet, salty, spicy Crispy Fried Noodles (*Mee Krob*; page 159) and the incomparable Thai Style Fried Noodles (*Phat Thai*; page 158)—are totally Thai. Both are usually found on the menus of Thai restaurants.

The simplicity of Thai soup noodle dishes, the complex fried varieties, and the rich stir-fried, gravy smothered dishes are all different and delicious. We hope it will not be too long before America discovers fresh Thai noodles, like it discovered fresh pasta, marking another step in the exploration of culinary geography.

♠ Plain Fried Rice
(Khaw Pat)

3 Tbsps vegetable oil

2 Tbsps finely chopped onion

1 Tbsp finely chopped garlic

5 cups cooked long-grain rice (one day old is best)

1 cup diced cooked chicken (again leftover is good)

2 eggs, lightly beaten

3 Tbsps fish soy (*nam pla*)

½ tsp white pepper

GARNISHES

1 Tbsp chopped fresh coriander leaves

1 cup sliced cucumber

2 Tbsps chopped red and green chili peppers

3 green onions, chopped

1 lime, cut into wedges

Heat the oil in a wok over medium-high heat. Add the onion and stir-fry 3 minutes; add the garlic and stir-fry until onion and garlic are golden. Add the rice and the diced chicken and stir-fry for 3 minutes. Add the beaten egg and stir vigorously until cooked. Sprinkle with fish soy and white pepper and remove from heat.

Place in a serving dish, add the GARNISHES, and serve hot.

♠ Coconut Rice
(Khaw Man)

This is served with any kind of curry, and, since it is richer than regular rice, people do not eat as much.

3 cups long-grain rice

4 cups coconut milk

1½ cups water

½ tsp salt

1 tsp sugar

Wash the rice well and drain it. Place in a heavy pot or rice cooker. Add the coconut milk, water, salt, and sugar and mix. Cover, bring to a rapid boil, and let it boil for 3–5 minutes. Reduce the heat to low and cook the rice for about 20 minutes, until done.

Richer flavors can be obtained by increasing the amount of coconut milk and decreasing the amount of water. For 3 cups rice, the total amount of liquid should be 5½ cups.

♠ Fried Rice with Shrimp Paste

SERVES 6–8

5 Tbsps vegetable oil
⅓ medium onion, cut into thin slices
2 Tbsps chopped garlic
1 Tbsp shrimp paste (*kapi*), flattened into a small pancake
¼ cup dried shrimp, rinsed and roughly chopped
juice of ½ lemon
4 cups cooked long-grain rice (slightly undercooked is best)

GARNISHES
2 eggs, well beaten (for egg shreds; see below)
2 Tbsps chopped fresh coriander leaves
¼ cup dried shrimp, chopped

CONDIMENTS
3 Tbsps chopped red chili peppers
1 cup thinly sliced cucumber
10 green onions, chopped

To make the egg shreds coat the bottom of a frying pan with 3 Tbsps oil and pour off the excess, retaining oil for next batch. Place over medium heat and add just enough of the beaten egg to cover the bottom. Fry until dry. Remove and repeat until the egg mixture is used up. Stack the egg sheets and cut them into fine shreds.

Put the remaining 2 Tbsps of oil in a frying pan over medium heat and add the onion. Stir-fry for 3 minutes, add the garlic, and stir-fry until onions and garlic are golden. Add the shrimp paste and ¼ cup dried shrimp and mix well. Mix in the lemon juice, increase heat to medium-high, and add the rice. Stir-fry until coated with shrimp paste and hot throughout.

Transfer the rice to a serving dish or individual plates and put all the GARNISHES on top—the egg shreds, coriander, and remaining ¼ cup of dried shrimp (chopped). Be sure that each portion includes some of each garnish. Place CONDIMENTS in small bowls and let each diner add what he or she likes.

♠ Classic Thai Fried Rice
(*Khaw Pat Thai*)

A small bowl of Chilies in Vinegar (see page 9) accompanies this dish, which is found everywhere in Thailand. This is almost a meal in itself. With a clear soup and a small salad, it becomes one.

SERVES 6–8

3 Tbsps vegetable oil
2 cloves garlic, crushed

2 tsps Red Curry Paste (see page 33)

5 oz (150 gm) pork shoulder, diced

4 cups cooked cold rice (leftover is fine, if it is not mushy)

2 Tbsps chopped dried shrimp

3 Tbsps fish soy (*nam pla*)

2 eggs, slightly beaten

1 green onion, chopped

1 Tbsp chopped fresh coriander leaves

GARNISHES

10 green onions

thin cucumber slices

Heat the oil in a frying pan or wok over medium-high heat. Add the garlic and stir-fry until it changes color. Add the curry paste and stir-fry until the aroma is released—a few seconds only—then add the pork shoulder and stir-fry for 3 more minutes.

Add the cold rice and stir-fry for 2 minutes, then add the dried shrimp.

Beat the fish soy into the eggs, and add this mixture to the rice. Continue to stir-fry until the eggs are set—about 3–5 minutes. Add the chopped green onion and coriander and transfer to a serving dish or individual plates.

Garnish with green onions that have been washed and soaked in ice water and with cucumber slices. (In Thailand green onion tops are shredded with a pin before they are plunged into the ice water. The cold curls them and makes an attractive garnish.)

▲ Fried Rice with Peppery Curry
(*Khaw Pat Prik King*)

SERVES 6–8

3 Tbsps vegetable oil

2 Tbsps finely chopped onion

1 Tbsp finely chopped garlic

½ cup dried (or cooked) shrimp

½ cup French-cut green beans

¼ lb (115 gm) shredded pork shoulder

2 Tbsps Peppery Curry Paste (see page 28)

5 cups cooked long-grain (or short-grain) rice

2 Tbsps fish soy (*nam pla*)

GARNISHES

1 Tbsp chopped fresh coriander leaves

½ cup thinly sliced cucumber

3 green onions, coarsely chopped

Heat the oil in a wok over medium-high heat. Add the finely chopped onion and stir-fry for 3 minutes, then add the garlic and stir-fry until both are golden. Add the dried shrimp, green beans, pork, and curry paste and stir-fry for 3 minutes. Add the cooked rice and fish soy and stir-fry until hot. Be careful not to overcook.

Place on a serving dish and arrange the coriander, cucumber, and green onion over the fried rice. Serve hot.

▲ Thai Style Fried Noodles
(Phat Thai)

SERVES 6–8

8 oz (225 gm) flat Thai noodles (*gwit dio*)
4 Tbsps vegetable oil
2 Tbsps chopped garlic
¼ lb (115 gm) ground pork

SEASONINGS
½ cup coarsely chopped or crushed peanuts
¼ cup dried shrimp
2 Tbsps chopped sweet pickled radish (any sweet
    pickled radish—Thai, Chinese, or Japanese)
¼ lb (115 gm) regular tofu (Japanese "cotton" tofu), cut
    into ½-inch (1-cm) cubes
2 Tbsps fish soy (*nam pla*)
2 tsps sugar
1 tsp red pepper flakes
juice of ½ lime (or lemon)
3 green onions, cut into 1-inch (2-cm) lengths

CONDIMENTS
1 cup bean sprouts
3 Tbsps fish soy (*nam pla*)
2 Tbsps finely slivered fresh red and green chili peppers
sugar (optional)
lime wedges

Boil noodles in ample lightly salted water for about 7 minutes or until al dente. Drain.

Heat the oil over medium heat in a wok or frying pan. Add the garlic and stir-fry until the color changes. Add the pork and stir-fry for 3–4 minutes. Add the noodles, stir well, and add all the SEASONINGS. Stir-fry for 5–7 minutes, being careful not to break the noodles.

Transfer to a serving dish and serve the CONDIMENTS in small dishes on the side. You might want to sprinkle some additional sugar on the noodles with the CONDIMENTS.

♠ Crispy Fried Noodles
(*Mee Krob*)

3–4 cups vegetable oil for deep-frying
4 oz (120 gm) rice vermicelli

SYRUP
¼ cup water
¼ cup tamarind water (see page 12) (or lime juice)
4 Tbsps sugar

SEASONINGS
¼ cup vegetable oil
2 Tbsps finely chopped onion
1 Tbsp finely chopped garlic
4 oz (120 gm) cooked ground pork
4 Tbsps chopped dried shrimp
1 Tbsp tomato paste
3 Tbsps fish soy (*nam pla*)

½ cup bean sprouts
1 Tbsp chopped fresh coriander leaves
2 green onions, cut into 1½-inch (4-cm) lengths
1 tsp red pepper flakes (optional)
6–8 lemon (or lime) wedges

Heat the oil to very hot (370° F/190° C). Drop a small handful of uncooked noodles into the hot oil. They will immediately puff up to several times their size. Turn the puffed noodles over and quickly fry the other side. The entire process only takes a few seconds. Do not let the noodles brown—they should be snowy white. Drain the fried noodles on paper toweling.

Make the SYRUP by combining the water and tamarind water (or lime juice) with sugar in a small saucepan. Cook over medium heat to make a syrup.

Prepare the SEASONINGS by heating the 1 Tbsp of vegetable oil in a frying pan. Add the onion and garlic and stir-fry until lightly browned. Add the ground pork, dried shrimp, and stir-fry 3–4 minutes. Add the tomato paste and fish soy and stir-fry 3 minutes more.

Clean the bean sprouts and remove the roots, if you like.

Place the noodles in a large bowl and pour the SYRUP and SEASONINGS mixtures over them at once and mix thoroughly with your hands. (This will, of course, be sticky.)

Add the bean sprouts, coriander, and green onion and mix again, being careful not to break the noodles into too small pieces. Sprinkle the red pepper flakes over the top if you like things hot and serve with the lemon or lime wedges. In Thailand this is always served with the tiny, fiery hot chili peppers (guinea peppers) known as *prik kee nu*.

This dish is slightly fussy to prepare, but it is worth it.

♠ Cold Noodles with Shrimp and Pineapple

(*Kanom Chine Sow Nam*)
(color page 19)

Traditionally, everything is served on separate dishes, and diners add whatever they like to the noodles. Here, the dish is adapted to serving family style.

SERVES 6

10-oz (300-gm) package Japanese thick *somen* noodles or *hiyamugi* noodles
½ fresh pineapple, coarsely chopped
2½ oz (75 gm) dried shrimp, rinsed
½ lb (225 gm) fresh medium shrimp, shelled, backs slit open, and deveined

SAUCE
3–4 Tbsps fish soy (*nam pla*)
1 cup coconut cream, boiled and cooled
juice of 1 lime
2 Tbsps sugar
2 Tbsps garlic oil (see page 10)

GARNISHES
3 green onions, chopped
2 tsps red pepper flakes
2 Tbsps chopped fresh coriander leaves
2 Tbsps finely chopped fresh ginger

Boil the noodles 2–3 minutes in ample water until al dente. Drain and plunge immediately into cold water. Drain again thoroughly. Spread the noodles on a large platter. Sprinkle chopped pineapple over the noodles.

In a mortar, pound the dried shrimp lightly and sprinkle it on the pineapple. Boil the fresh shrimp for 1 minute. Cool, chop, and spread over the dried shrimp.

Mix the SAUCE ingredients and pour over the noodles. Sprinkle with the green onion, red pepper flakes, coriander leaves, and ginger.

You can substitute a large can of pineapple tidbits (drained) for the fresh pineapple.

♠ Fried Noodles with Spinach

This is a splendid accompaniment to western roasts or fowl—a welcome change from potatoes or rice.

SERVES 6–8

2 lbs (1 kg) flat Thai noodles (*gwit dio*)
10-oz (300-gm) package frozen spinach (or 1 lb/450 gm fresh spinach)
4 Tbsps vegetable oil (or butter)
1 Tbsp finely chopped garlic

2 Tbsps fish soy (*nam pla*)

½ tsp pepper

Boil the noodles in an ample amount of lightly salted water for 7 minutes or until al dente. Drain.

Cook the fresh or frozen spinach until tender, drain, and chop finely.

Melt the oil (or butter) in a large frying pan over medium heat and fry the garlic until the color changes. Add the cooked noodles and stir-fry for 5 minutes. Add all remaining ingredients and stir-fry an additional 5 minutes, taking care not to break the noodles.

Serve hot.

♨Thai Style Soup Noodles
(*Gwit Dio Nam*)

For this recipe almost any kind of noodle will do—rice noodles, egg noodles. Even instant ramen is good served this way.

SERVES 6–8

1 lb (450 gm) fresh or dried noodles

8½ cups well-flavored chicken stock (see page 12)

½ cup julienned celery

4 Tbsps fish soy (*nam pla*)

2 cups cooked chicken, beef, pork, or shrimp cut into thin bite-sized pieces

2 green onions, cut into 1½-inch (4-cm) lengths

2 Tbsps chopped fresh coriander leaves

2 Tbsps garlic oil (see page 10)

2 Tbsps Chinese pickle (Tientsin Preserved Vegetable)

CONDIMENTS

red pepper flakes

fish soy (*nam pla*)

vinegar (or lime or lemon juice)

Boil noodles in an ample amount of water, stirring constantly, until they are al dente. Drain.

Bring the 8½ cups chicken stock to a boil and add the celery and fish soy. Season to taste.

Divide the hot noodles into 6–8 deep soup bowls and then divide the meat or shrimp and onions, coriander, garlic oil, and Chinese pickle into the appropriate number of portions and put on the noodles. Pour the chicken stock over the noodles in the bowls.

Each diner seasons the broth with red pepper flakes, fish soy, and vinegar (or lime or lemon juice).

▲ Noodles with Spareribs

6 oz (180 gm) rice vermicelli or flat Thai noodles (*gwit dio*)

CHILI SAUCE
½ cup rice vinegar
2 tsps sugar
1 Tbsp fish soy (*nam pla*)
chopped fresh red and green chili peppers to taste

1⅔ lbs (750 gm) spareribs cut into 1½-inch (4-cm) pieces
(ask the butcher to do this)

SEASONINGS
4 Tbsps fish soy (*nam pla*)
1 slice fresh (or dried) galanga
1 stalk celery, cut into 1½-inch (4-cm) lengths
2 cloves garlic
2 Tbsps chopped onion
3 thin slices fresh ginger

CONDIMENTS
2 Tbsps chopped fresh coriander leaves
2 Tbsps garlic oil (see page 10)
3 green onions, cut into 1½-inch (4-cm) lengths

Pour boiling water over the rice vermicelli and soak it for 10 minutes (or boil the Thai flat noodles for 7 minutes).

Prepare the CHILI SAUCE by combining the vinegar, sugar, fish soy, and chili peppers. Set aside for 1 hour (keeps for up to 1 month in the refrigerator).

Place the sparerib pieces in a pressure cooker with 6 cups of water. Add all the SEASONINGS, cover, and bring to a boil over high heat. Reduce the heat to low and cook for 20 minutes. Turn the heat off and let cool for at least 10 minutes—until no pressure remains—before opening the pressure cooker. (Or, simmer covered, for about 1 hour in a soup pot.)

Strain the sparerib broth into a saucepan and set the spareribs aside. If you prefer, you can cut the meat off the bones. Bring the stock to a boil again and adjust the seasonings.

Divide the noodles into individual bowls. Arrange the spareribs on top of the noodles and pour the hot broth over.

Place the CONDIMENTS and CHILI SAUCE on the table and let people help themselves.

VARIATION
Use 4 cups of hot boiled rice instead of noodles.

▲ Noodles with Pork and Bean Sprouts

1½ cups bean sprouts

6 packages instant ramen (discard any seasonings contained in ramen packets)

1 lb (450 gm) cooked pork (or beef, chicken), cut into thin bite-sized pieces

3 green onions, chopped

3 Tbsps Chinese pickle (Tientsin Preserved Vegetable)

½ cup peanuts, coarsely chopped or crushed

CONDIMENTS

lemon wedges

fish soy (*nam pla*)

garlic oil (see page 10)

sugar

Wash the bean sprouts (discard any brown seed cases), remove roots, if desired, place in a bowl, and pour boiling water over them. Leave for only 1 minute and immediately refresh in cold water.

Bring an ample amount of water to a boil in a large pot, add the noodles, cook for 3–4 minutes, and drain.

Divide the hot noodles into individual bowls and arrange portions of meat, green onion, bean sprouts, Chinese pickle, and crushed peanuts over them.

Each diner adds his/her own CONDIMENTS (some of each) and then mixes the noodles before eating.

▲ Smothered Noodles
(*Gwit Dio Raht Na*)

1¾ lbs (800 gm) fresh (or dried) flat Thai noodles (*gwit dio*)
(or 10 oz/300 gm rice vermicelli)

⅔ lb (300 gm) pork roast, thinly sliced

1 Tbsp saké

½ lb (225 gm) broccoli

SEASONINGS

1 Tbsp brown salty bean paste (Chinese or Japanese)

3 Tbsps cornstarch dissolved in 4 Tbsps water

1 Tbsp sugar

1 Tbsp fish soy (*nam pla*)

½ tsp freshly ground black pepper

½ tsp salt

¾ cup vegetable oil

3 Tbsps thick Chinese soy sauce (substitute regular soy sauce)

1 Tbsp chopped garlic

5 oz (150 gm) fresh shrimp, shelled, slit down the backs, and deveined, with tails intact

If using rice vermicelli, soak it in boiling water for 10 minutes and drain. If you are fortunate enough to find fresh Thai noodles, use them as is. (It is also possible to use Japanese instant ramen, which is readily available.)

Cut the sliced pork into 1 × 2-inch (2 × 5-cm) pieces and marinate it in the saké for 5 minutes. Discard broccoli leaves and peel stem skin if it is tough. Cut the broccoli into small florets and slice the stems.

Blend all the SEASONINGS.

Heat ¼ cup of the vegetable oil in a wok over high heat. Add the drained (or fresh) noodles and the thick Chinese soy sauce. Stir-fry the noodles for 3 minutes. Remove noodles to individual serving plates. Keep warm.

Add the remaining ½ cup of oil to the wok over medium-high heat, then add the chopped garlic. Stir-fry until it is golden, add the pork, and stir-fry for 2 minutes. Now add the shrimp, broccoli, and SEASONINGS mixture along with 2½ cups of boiling water. Stir-fry for 3 minutes, until sauce thickens. Divide the sauce evenly over the noodles. Serve with Chilies in Vinegar (page 9).

SWEETS

ของหวาน

As in many Asian nations, in Thailand the names of things are considered to have importance. Many sweets and confections, thus, have names that are propitious and that evoke good fortune and happiness, names especially fitting for special occasions and events such as weddings and birthday celebrations.

Thai sweets, in general, are made from a limited number of ingredients, and preparation in the traditional manner is often a major effort. Fortunately, modern appliances have simplified this to a great extent. The first impression many westerners have of Thai sweets is of coconut-flavored paste. This is because coconut, coconut milk, and various starches (which are usually steamed) play a major role. Sweets are prepared by steaming, frying, stewing, and (recently) baking.

Thailand has some of the best fruit in the world. In Thailand, perhaps more popular than sweet confections are sweet fruits—nature's bounty.

♠ Golden Thai Cookies
(*Tong Ek*)

2 cups raw sugar (substitute brown sugar)
1½ cups thick coconut milk
5 oz (150 gm) roasted unsalted cashews
8 egg yolks
¼ tsp jasmine essence
pinch of salt

Dissolve the sugar in the coconut milk over medium heat. Let it cool.

If the unsalted cashews are raw, roast them on a cookie sheet in a medium-hot oven until they turn light gold. Cool, then whir them in a blender or food processor until very fine. Add to the cooled coconut milk mixture. Add the egg yolks, jasmine essence, and salt and cook over low heat, stirring constantly, until thick. Turn the heat off and continue stirring until the batter becomes thick (like bread dough).

Spread on a buttered platter to ¼-inch (¾-cm) thickness. Smooth the top and cut into fancy shapes with cookie cutters (the smaller the better, since these are very rich).

The cookies will keep 2–3 weeks in an airtight container.

♠ Bananas in Coconut Cream
(*Gluay Baud Chee*)
(color page 20)

6 firm, underripe bananas

SAUCE
2 cups coconut cream
½ cup raw (or brown) sugar
¼ tsp salt
¼ tsp jasmine (or rose) essence

GARNISH
2 Tbsps white sesame seeds, toasted (see page 11)

Peel the greenest bananas you can find, split them lengthwise as for a banana split, and cut each half into 4 pieces.

Mix the SAUCE ingredients with 1 cup of water, add the banana chunks, and bring to a gentle boil. Reduce the heat to low and cook for 5 minutes. (If the bananas are not green enough, they tend to get mushy.)

Put in individual bowls or one large bowl, sprinkle with toasted sesame seeds, and serve hot.

▲ Thai Tapioca Pudding
(*Saku Peek*)

SERVES 6–8

3 cups coconut milk
¾ cup small pearl tapioca
pinch of salt
1½ cups powdered sugar (or 1 cup raw sugar)
2 eggs, separated
2 Tbsps powdered sugar

GARNISHES
¼ cup peanuts, coarsely chopped or crushed
8 candied or maraschino cherries, chopped

Put the coconut milk, tapioca, salt, and 1½ cups powdered sugar in a saucepan. Simmer over low heat, stirring constantly, for 10 minutes or until tapioca is clear. Remove from heat and add the egg yolks. Blend well.

Beat the 2 egg whites until stiff but not dry. Fold in the 2 Tbsps of powdered sugar and the tapioca mixture. Put in 6–8 dessert dishes. Sprinkle with crushed peanuts and chopped cherries. Serve hot or cold.

▲ Steamed Coconut Cups
(*Kanom Talai*)

MAKES 15 CUPS

DARK MIXTURE
2 cups coconut milk
1 cup rice flour
¾ cup raw sugar (substitute brown sugar)
pinch of salt

LIGHT MIXTURE
1 cup thick coconut cream
2 Tbsps raw sugar (or regular sugar)
2 Tbsps rice flour
pinch of salt

Blend the ingredients for the DARK MIXTURE well and fill 15 large (½-cup) foil cups half full. Steam over medium heat for 20 minutes or until the mixture is set.

Blend the ingredients for the LIGHT MIXTURE and put 2 Tbsps in each foil cup. Steam 25 minutes more or until it appears dry on top. Cool and run a knife around the foil cup to facilitate removal. Serve cool or at room temperature with the light side up.

♠ Glutinous Rice with Mangoes
(*Khaw Neaw Mamuang*)

SERVES 6–8

3 cups glutinous rice

SEASONINGS
1½ cups coconut cream
½ cup sugar
1 tsp salt

SAUCE
1¼ cups thick coconut cream
2 Tbsps sugar
¼ tsp salt

5–6 ripe mangoes, well chilled

GARNISH
2 Tbsps toasted sesame seeds (or chopped cashews)

Soak the glutinous rice in ample cold water for 2 hours. Drain well. Line a steamer with cheesecloth, heat steamer, spread the glutinous rice on the cheesecloth, and steam for 30 minutes or until cooked through. The rice will become glossy.

Mix the SEASONINGS ingredients in a large bowl and gently mix in the hot steamed rice. Cover tightly and let soak for 30 minutes to absorb the coconut flavor.

Blend the thick coconut cream, sugar, and salt in a saucepan and heat it just to the boiling point. Turn the heat off and let the SAUCE cool.

Peel the well-chilled mangoes, slice lengthwise, and remove the seeds.

Divide the rice among 6–8 plates. Place the chilled mango slices on top and cover with the SAUCE. Sprinkle with toasted sesame seeds and serve.

♠ Golden Split Pea Cake
(*Kanom mo Gang*)

MAKES 25 PIECES

4 cups yellow split peas
8 eggs
5 Tbsps flour
½ tsp salt
2½ cups raw sugar (substitute regular sugar)
3 cups thick coconut cream

GARNISHES
1 cup thinly sliced onion
½ cup vegetable oil

Wash the split peas, soak them for 2 hours in enough warm water to cover, drain, and then steam them over medium heat for 30 minutes. Place the peas in a food processor and blend to a coarse paste.

In a large saucepan, beat the 8 eggs well and mix in the flour, salt, sugar, coconut cream, and split pea paste. Stir over low heat until thick, then pour into a greased 13½ × 8¾-inch (30 × 20-cm) shallow pan. Place this pan in a shallow pan of hot water (*bain marie*) in the oven. Bake in a moderate (350°F/175°C) oven for 1 hour or until a skewer or cake tester comes out clean.

While the cake is baking, fry the thinly sliced onion in the vegetable oil until golden. Sprinkle the fried onion over the cake immediately after it comes out of the oven. Let the cake cool before cutting it into about 25 pieces.

⚜ Steamed Custard in Winter Squash
(*Sang Ka Ya Fak Tong*)
(color page 20)

The small pumpkinlike Japanese kabocha *squash have an excellent flavor and the perfect shape for this attractive dessert. You can even eat the skin. If* kabocha *squash are not available, use acorn squash or small Hubbard squash (or any winter squash you like) and cut and seed it so that the squash will act as a receptacle for the custard and remain stable.*

SERVES 8–10

1 medium (9-inch/23-cm diameter) Japanese *kabocha* squash
   or one large acorn squash

CUSTARD
4 eggs, well beaten
1 cup coconut milk
½ cup raw sugar
3 drops jasmine essence
pinch of salt

Wash the squash but do not peel it. Cut off the top, remove the seeds, and wash and dry the inside thoroughly.

Blend the egg, coconut milk, sugar, jasmine essence, and salt.

Place the winter squash in a heatproof bowl that will hold it perfectly straight. Fill the squash with the CUSTARD mixture and steam over medium heat for 1½ hours. It is done when the flesh is tender when pricked with a skewer. Cool to room temperature before cutting into 8 or 10 wedges. Eat both the squash and the custard.

This can be prepared and refrigerated 1 or 2 days before serving. It is not necessary to bring it to room temperature—it is equally delicious chilled.

♠ Coconut Cakes
(*Kanom Klok*)

Although it seems odd, newly harvested rice does not work in this very traditional Thai sweet—it is best if the rice has been sitting around for a year or more. In Thailand, chives are added to these cakes, but the result is not particularly pleasing to the western palate.

MAKES ABOUT 30 2-INCH (5-CM) PIECES

2 cups OLD raw long-grain rice
¾ cup cooked long-grain rice
1½ cups grated coconut (fresh or dried)
1 tsp salt

TOPPING
2¼ cups coconut cream
¾ cup sugar
1½ tsps salt

In a large mixing bowl add 6 cups of boiling water to the 2 cups of old raw rice and ¾ cup of cooked rice. Stir constantly and quickly until the mixture cools. This constant stirring prevents the boiling water from cooking the raw rice. Add the grated coconut and 1 tsp of salt. Make a sticky dough of the mixture in a blender, food processor, or mortar and pestle.

Prepare the TOPPING by dissolving the sugar and salt in the coconut cream.

A special pan with half-spherical forms is used to make *Kanom Klok*. A Danish *aebleskiver* (apple dumpling) pan will do very well.

Fill each of the hollows three-fourths full of the sticky mixture and fill to the top with the TOPPING. Cover with a lid (or foil) and cook over medium heat for about 3 minutes. If they are bubbling in the middle, they are done. Remove the cakes with a soup spoon and repeat until all the batter is used. Serve hot.

Westerners can add a familiar touch with a sprinkle of cinnamon and sugar.

♠ Three-Color Glutinous Rice Balls
(*Kanom Tom Sam Si*)
(color page 20)

MAKES ABOUT 30 BALLS

3 cups glutinous rice flour (Japanese: *shiratamako*)
2 Tbsps white sesame seeds, toasted
pinch of salt
¼ tsp jasmine extract (substitute vanilla)

1¼ cups water
green and red food coloring
½ cup raw sugar
½ cup finely chopped peanuts (or ½ cup grated fresh [or angel-flake] coconut)
pinch of salt

COATING
½ cup grated fresh (or angel-flake) coconut
½ cup white sesame seeds, toasted
½ cup sugar

Mix the glutinous rice flour, 2 Tbsps white sesame seeds, and pinch of salt and divide it into 3 equal parts.

Mix the jasmine extract (or vanilla) with the 1¼ cups water and divide it into three parts. Tint one part pink, one part green, and leave the last one uncolored. Add one part of the water to one part of the flour mixture and mix until the dough is uniform. Knead each ball (the pink, green, and white) for 5 minutes in its bowl. Form each dough color into 1-inch (2-cm) balls. You should have 10 balls of each color.

Crush the raw sugar with a rolling pin and mix it with the peanuts (or grated coconut). Make a hole in each of the balls, insert about ⅓ tsp of the sugar-peanut (or -coconut) mixture in each hole, and form into smooth balls again.

Bring 6 cups of water with ½ tsp salt to a boil over high heat. Add about half the rice balls at once and cook until they float to the top. Remove, drain, and cool.

Mix the COATING ingredients. Roll the balls in this mixture until uniformly covered. Arrange attractively on a serving plate. Sprinkle with any remaining COATING mixture.

▲ Glutinous Rice and Bananas
(*Khaw Tom Pat*)
(color page 20)

Traditionally this dessert is wrapped in banana leaves. If you have a banana tree in your garden and want to try, trim off the center vein and use 6 × 8-inch (15 × 20-cm) pieces of green leaf instead of foil.

MAKES 20 SERVINGS

3 cups glutinous rice
1 cup azuki beans, soaked overnight in cold water
3 cups coconut milk
2 tsps salt
⅔ cup sugar
5 bananas
20 6 × 8-inch (15 × 20-cm) pieces foil

Wash the glutinous rice. Cover with 10 cups of water and soak for at least 6 hours or overnight. Drain.

Simmer the azuki beans in 3 cups water over medium-low heat in a partially covered saucepan for about 40 minutes. Cook until they are just tender, not mushy.

Put the coconut milk in a large saucepan. Add the salt and sugar and bring to a boil over medium heat. Add the well-drained glutinous rice, and cook, stirring constantly, until all the coconut milk is absorbed—about 15 minutes.

Cut the bananas into halves lengthwise then cut these in half crosswise. Put 2 Tbsps of glutinous rice in the middle (the long way) of each piece of foil. Flatten the rice and place a banana quarter on top. Arrange cooked azuki beans around the edge of the banana on the rice, then cover with an additional 2 Tbsps glutinous rice. Flatten it to cover the banana. Bring the two long sides of foil up to meet above the rice. Fold twice and press down on rice. Fold both ends up and over and press down to make a neat, even package. Steam over medium heat for 20–25 minutes. Serve in the wrapper warm or at room temperature.

ARIZONA

Kimbong Market
502 S. Dobson Rd.
Mesa, AZ 85202

Siam Import Market
5008 W. Northern Ave., Suite 3
Glendale, AZ 85301

CALIFORNIA

Southern

Ai Hoa Supermarket
860 N. Hill St.
Los Angeles, CA 90012

American-Chinese Market
1609 W. 7th St.
Los Angeles, CA 90017

Asian Food Mart
12311 Westminster Ave.
Santa Ana, CA 92703

A. V. Oriental Food Market
1837 Avenue I
Lancaster, CA 93534

Bangkok Market
4804-06 Melrose Ave.
Los Angeles, CA 90029

B & B (Atlantic) Market
10427-9 Atlantic Ave.
South Gate, CA 90280

Hoa Binh Market
437 E. Holt Ave.
Pomona, CA 91767

Indra Market
4668 Verdugo Rd.
Glendale, CA 90065

J. P. Market
974 S. Western Ave.
Los Angeles, CA 90006

Jackpot Market
2309 Pacific Coast Hwy.
Long Beach, CA 90804

Kim Hoa Oriental Market
7227 DeSoto Ave.
Canoga Park, CA 91306

Lane Xang Market
13281-85 Brookhurst
Garden Grove, CA 92643

L. A. Supermarket
675 N. Spring St.
Los Angeles, CA 90012

Lynwood Market
11325 Atlantic Ave.
Lynwood, CA 90262

Man Wah Supermarket
758-762 New High St.
Los Angeles, CA 90012

Minimart People
8652-54 Woodman Ave.
Arleta, CA 91331

Neighborhood Market
9734 Artesia Blvd.
Bellflower, CA 90706

Oriental Mart
11827 Del Amo Blvd.
Cerritos, CA 90701

Oriental Grocery
5527 Del Amo Blvd.
Lakewood, CA 90712

Oriental Supermarket
9874 Garden Grove Blvd.
Garden Grove, CA 92664

Pantai Oriental Food Inc.
1750 Albion St.
Los Angeles, CA 90031

Smart Market
8236 Coldwater Canyon
North Hollywood, CA 91605

Spisook Oriental Food
1200 E. Highland Ave., Suite E
San Bernadino, CA 92404

Sunshine Market
3345 E. Artesia Blvd.
Long Beach, CA 90805

Thai Food Market
5902-4 Hollywood Blvd.
Hollywood, CA 90028

Vienchan Market
207 N. Western Ave.
Los Angeles, CA 90004

Viet Hoa Supermarket
211 Alpine St., No. 1
Los Angeles, CA 90012

Viet Hoa Supermarket
2309 Pacific Coast Hwy.
Long Beach, CA 90804

Wai Wai Supermarket
3969 Beverly Blvd.
Los Angeles, CA 90004

Northern

Bankgok Grocery
3226 Geary Blvd.
San Francisco, CA 94118

Siam West Oriental Groceries
9234 Petaluma Hill Road
Santa Rosa, CA 95404

Thai Market
3826 Westlane
Stockton, CA 95204

Thai Store
969 Grand Ave.
San Rafael, CA 94901

Valley Market
1763 Chestnut St.
Livermore, CA 94550

Vientiane Market
233 Jones St.
San Francisco, CA 94102

COLORADO

Coronado Liquor
1991 Coronado Pky.
Thornton, CO 80229

K Grocery
4966 Leetsdale
Denver, CO 80222

Krung Thai Grocery
10146 Montiview Blvd.
Aurora, CO 80010

Oriental Food Market
2907 Arapahoe
Boulder, CO 80302

Thai Grocery 1
1001 S. Federal Blvd.
Denver, CO 80219

Thai Grocery 2
8141 Colfax Ave.
Denver, CO 80220

FLORIDA

Asian Market
3214 9th St.
St. Petersburg, FL

Far East Grocery
14616 66th St.
Clearwater, FL 33546

International Market
1033 9th St.
St. Petersburg, FL

Peter Oriental Imports
3490 57th St.
St. Petersburg, FL

Siam Inc.
591 E. Semoran Blvd.
Casselberry, FL 32707

Siam Market
3611 S. Dale Mabry Hwy.
Tampa, FL 33609

Thai Center
737 9th St.
Sialeah, FL 33010

Thai Market
916 Harrelson St.
Ft. Walton Beach, FL 32548

Thai Market
41110 West Highway 95
Panama City, FL 32405

Thai Market
3323-25 S. Dale Mabry Hwy.
Tampa, FL 33609

Tampa Oriental Supermarket
6002 S. Dale Mabry Hwy.
Tampa, FL 33611

GEORGIA

Asia Grocery
7984 N. Main St.
Jonesboro, GA 30236

Lim's Oriental Food and Gift
4887 Memorial Div. Stone Min.
Atlanta, GA 30319

Thai Oriental Market
6467 Highway 85
Riverdale, GA 30274

HAWAII

Asia Grocery
1362 S. Beretania St.
Honolulu, Hawaii 96814

Siam Panich Grocery
171 N. Beretania St.
Honolulu, Hawaii 96813

ILLINOIS

Anou Oriental Food Ltd.
1423 8th St.
Rockford, IL.

Bangkok Grocery
1003-5 W. Leland Ave.
Chicago, IL

Chiengmai Grocery
3134 W. Lawrence Ave.
Chicago, IL

Rama Market
4611 N. Sheridan Rd.
Chicago, IL

Suda's Grocery
6430 N. Western Ave.
Chicago, IL 60659

Thai Grocery
5014-16 N. Broadway Ave.
Chicago, IL

Thai Market
4654 N. Western Ave.
Chicago, IL

Thai Oriental Grocery
5124 S. Kedzie
Chicago, IL 60632

Thai Oriental Mart
1656 S. 55th St.
Chicago, IL 60615

Thailand Plaza
1135-37 W. Argyle
Chicago, IL 60640

INDIANA

N. P. Asia Food
3737 N. Shadeland Ave.
Indianapolis, IN 46226

MICHIGAN

Siam Thai Import Market
17626 Lasher Ave.
Detriot, MI 48219

MINNESOTA

Thai Store
1304 Eastlake St.
Minneapolis, MN 55407

MISSISSIPPI

Oriental Mart
2856-D Pass Rd.
Biloxi, MS 39531

MISSOURI

Asian Market
2601 Independence Ave.
Kansas City, MO 64124

Jay Asia Food
3232 S. Grand St.
St. Louis, MO 63118

NEBRASKA

Asian Market
2413 Lincoln Rd.
Bellevue, NE 68005

Bangkok Oriental Market
645 S. Locwt (sic) (Locust?)
Grand Island, NE 68801

Siam Market
213 W. Mission Ave.
Omaha, NE 68005

NEVADA

Asia Market
1101 E. Charleston Blvd.
Las Vegas, NV 89104

Internation Market
900 E. Karen Ave.
Las Vegas, NV 89104

NEW YORK

Bangkok Market
106 Park St.
New York, NY 10013

Phuping Thai Grocery
81-A Bayard St.
Chinatown, NY 10013

Siam Grocery
2754 Broadway
New York, NY 10025

Taksin Grocery
857 9th Ave
New York, NY 10019

Thai Market
157-A E. 170th St.
The Bronx, NY 10452

NORTH CAROLINA

Thai Market Inc.
122-24 S. Main St.
Spring Lake, NC 28390

OHIO

Bangkok Grocery and Gift Store
3277 Refugee Rd.
Columbus, OH 43227

Laovieng Store
1511 E. Livingston Ave.
Columbus, OH 43205

Thai Grocery
108 E. Main St.
Columbus, OH 43215

OKLAHOMA

Su's Oriental Market
3313 E. 32nd Pl.
Tulsa, OK

Thai Grocery
1001 S. Federal Blvd.
Oklahoma City, OK

OREGON

Rama Market
7901 S.E. Stark St.
Portland, OR 97215

PENNSYLVANIA

P & P Grocery
4307 Locus St.
Philadelphia, PA 19104

SOUTH CAROLINA

Port of Siam
5400 Hwy. AS (sic)
Myrtle Beach, SC 29577

TEXAS

American-Asian Foods
6866 Shady Brook Ln.
Dallas, TX

A. P. Oriental Market
3835 Chester Boyer Rd.
Ft. Worth, TX 76103

Asian Grocery-Gift
121 Ave. A
Denton, TX 76201

Asian Grocery
9191 Forest Lane
Dallas, TX 75243

Bangkok Market
3404 Navigation
Houston, TX

Dragon Gate Market
3524 E. Lancaster
Ft. Worth, TX 76103

Loas Grocery
5813 Amarillo Blvd. E (sic)
Amarillo, TX 79107

Oriental Market
114 Northwood Shopping Center
Greenville at Forest Lane
Dallas, TX 75243

Singha Siam Grocery
2636 N. Fitzhugh
Dallas, TX 75204

Thai Kitchen and Grocery
9150-A S. Main
Houston, TX 77025

Thailand Market
2216 Grau Way
Irving, TX 75061

UTAH

Royal Thai Market
860 W. Riverdale Rd.
Riverdale City, UT 84403

WASHINGTON

Angor Wat Market
5912 196th St.
Lynwood, WA 98036

Asian Market
10855 N.E. 8th St.
Bellevue, WA 98004

Bangkok Jame
1412 3rd Ave.
Seattle, WA 98101

Crist's Import Mart
1367 B & C Geo Washington Way
Richland, WA 99352

Ding Hao Market
29100 Pacific Highway S
Federal Way, WA 98003

Grand Palace
31205 Pacific Highway S
Federal Way, WA 98003

Pou Thai Markets
2824 Empire Way 50 S
Seattle, WA

Rainier Oriental Food & Gifts
2919 Rainier Ave. S
Seattle, WA 98144

WASHINGTON, D.C., AREA

Asian Foods Inc.
2301 University Blvd. W
Wheaton, MD 20902

Asian-American Grocery
8236 Georgia Ave.
Silver Spring, MD 20910

Asian-American Bangkok
Grocery
412-A Hungerford Dr.
Rockville, MD 20850

Backlick Oriental Food Market
6681-82 Backlick Rd.
Springfield, VA 22150

Bangkok Oriental Food
4917 Suitland Rd.
Suitland, MD 20746

Bangkok '54 Oriental Food
3832 Mt. Vernon Ave.
Alexandria, VA 22305

CNC International
9317 Livingston Rd.
Oxon Hill, MD 20744

Duangrat Oriental Food Mart
5888 Leesburg Pike
Falls Church, VA 22041

Thai House Grocery
1733 Wilson Blvd.
Arlington, VA 22209

Thai Market Inc.
902 Thayer Ave.
Silver Spring, MD 20910

Thai Oriental Market
4807-9 Columbia Pike
Arlington, VA 22204

WISCONSIN

Oriental Grocery
322 E. Main St.
Waukesha, WI 53186

Vientiance Market
12205 16th St.
Milwaukee, WI 53204

INDEX